乔布斯自述

STEVEN JOBS 1955—2011

史蒂夫·乔布斯◎著　巨澜 李墨林◎译

S

O

J

B

中国时代经济出版社

CONTENTS 目录

序：追忆

A Sister's Eulogy
for Steve Jobs

劳伦、丽萨、和史蒂夫　　　Laurene, Lisa and Steve

2003年，史蒂夫、伊芙、里德、埃琳和劳伦在意大利的拉维罗

SJ, Eve, Reed, Erin and Laurene in Ravello, Italy

A Sister's Eulogy for Steve Jobs

By MONA SIMPSON,
New York Times,
October 30, 2011

I grew up as an only child, with a single mother. Because we were poor and because I knew my father had emigrated from Syria, I imagined he looked like Omar Sharif. I hoped he would be rich and kind and would come into our lives (and our not yet furnished apartment) and help us. Later, after I'd met my father, I tried to believe he'd changed his number and left no forwarding address because he was an idealistic revolutionary, plotting a new world for the Arab people

Even as a feminist, my whole life I'd been waiting for a man to love, who could love me. For decades, I'd thought that man would be my father. When I was 25, I met that man and he was my brother.

By then, I lived in New York, where I was trying to write my first novel. I had a job at a small magazine in an office the size of a closet, with three other aspiring writers. When one day a lawyer called me — me, the middle-class girl from California who hassled the boss to buy us health insurance — and said his client was rich and famous and was my long-lost brother, the young editors went wild. This was 1985 and we worked at a cutting-edge literary magazine, but I'd fallen into the plot of a Dickens novel and really, we all loved those best. The lawyer refused to tell me my brother's name and my colleagues started a betting pool. The leading candidate: John Travolta. I secretly hoped for a literary descendant of

追 忆

莫娜·辛普森
《纽约时报》
2011年10月30日

　　我从小跟着母亲在单亲家庭长大，因为日子过得拮据，加上父亲又是叙利亚移民，所以我一幻想着他能有奥玛·沙里夫一样的容貌，富有而慈祥，有朝一日能出现在我们的生活中（不嫌弃我们家徒四壁的房子），帮帮我们娘俩。后来，我终于见到了他，我还尽量让自己相信，他之所以换了电话号码甚至连个寄信地址都没有留下，是因为他是个理想主义革命者，正为阿拉伯人民规划着新的世界。

　　即便我是个女权主义者，在我整个人生中，也都在期盼着能有一个我爱的且也爱的我男人出现，二十年多年来，我一直觉得这个男人应该是我的父亲，而在我二十五岁的时候，终于遇到了这样的一个男人 —— 我的哥哥。

　　那时候，我住在纽约，正在埋头撰写我的第一本小说。我在一家小杂志社上班，办公室小得像衣橱一样，还有三个同事，也都是心怀理想的作家。一天，我接到了一位律师打来的电话 —— 我，一个来自加利福尼亚中产家庭的，整天吵着让老板给我们上健康保险的女孩 —— 律师说他的委托人是位有名的富翁，居然是我失散多年的哥哥，那些年轻的编辑们听到都疯掉了。那是1985年，我们供职的是一家先锋文学杂志，可狄更斯小说中的情节却突然出现在了我的生活中，我们所有人都乐坏了。律师拒

Henry James — someone more talented than I, someone brilliant without even trying.

When I met Steve, he was a guy my age in jeans, Arab- or Jewish-looking and handsomer than Omar Sharif.

We took a long walk — something, it happened, that we both liked to do. I don't remember much of what we said that first day, only that he felt like someone I'd pick to be a friend. He explained that he worked in computers.

I didn't know much about computers. I still worked on a manual Olivetti typewriter.

I told Steve I'd recently considered my first purchase of a computer: something called the Cromemco.

Steve told me it was a good thing I'd waited. He said he was making something that was going to be insanely beautiful.

I want to tell you a few things I learned from Steve, during three distinct periods, over the 27 years I knew him. They're not periods of years, but of states of being. His full life. His illness. His dying.

Steve worked at what he loved. He worked really hard. Every day.

That's incredibly simple, but true.

He was the opposite of absent-minded.

He was never embarrassed about working hard, even if the results were failures. If someone as smart as Steve wasn't ashamed to admit trying, maybe I didn't have to be.

When he got kicked out of Apple, things were painful. He told me about a dinner at which 500 Silicon

绝告诉我哥哥的名字，于是我的同事们开始打赌猜测起来，票数最多的候选人是约翰·特拉沃尔塔，我却暗自幻想着会是亨利·詹姆斯的文学弟子——比我出色，不需努力，也会才华横溢的人。

我第一次见到史蒂夫的时候，发现他和我年纪相仿，穿着牛仔裤，有一张阿拉伯或者犹太人的面孔，比奥玛·沙里夫英俊。

我们一起散步，走了很远——我们俩都喜欢散步。至于我们见面第一天都谈了些什么，我已经不太记得了，只记得我们像是相识已久的老朋友，他说他从事的是计算机方面的工作。

我当时对计算机还知之甚少，使用的还是Olivetti打字机。我告诉史蒂夫我最近正考虑买一台Cromemco计算机。

史蒂夫说，这个东西还算不错，而他正在研发一台超级美好的电脑。

我想告诉各位一些我从史蒂夫那里学到的东西，在我们相处的二十七年中，大致可以分为三个阶段。我说的并不是年份上的时期，而是生活状态上的阶段——他充实的生活，他的疾病以及他的离去。

史蒂夫热爱他的工作，而且非常努力，天天如此。

说起来简单得令人难以置信，但确实如此。

他从来不会心不在焉。

他努力工作，不在乎结果如何，即便最后失败，也不

Valley leaders met the then-sitting president. Steve hadn't been invited.

He was hurt but he still went to work at NeXT. Every single day.

Novelty was not Steve's highest value. Beauty was.

For an innovator, Steve was remarkably loyal. If he loved a shirt, he'd order 10 or 100 of them. In the Palo Alto house, there are probably enough black cotton turtlenecks for everyone in this church.

He didn't favor trends or gimmicks. He liked people his own age.

His philosophy of aesthetics reminds me of a quote that went something like this: "Fashion is what seems beautiful now but looks ugly later; art can be ugly at first but it becomes beautiful later."

Steve always aspired to make beautiful later.

He was willing to be misunderstood.

Uninvited to the ball, he drove the third or fourth iteration of his same black sports car to NeXT, where he and his team were quietly inventing the platform on which Tim Berners-Lee would write the program for the World Wide Web.

Steve was like a girl in the amount of time he spent talking about love. Love was his supreme virtue, his god of gods. He tracked and worried about the romantic lives of the people working with him.

Whenever he saw a man he thought a woman might find dashing, he called out, "Hey are you single? Do you wanna come to dinner with my sister?"

I remember when he phoned the day he met

会觉得尴尬。如果换成我，即便是能和史蒂夫一样聪明，也未必能做到如此。

他离开苹果的时候，很痛苦。他告诉我说当时美国总统设宴招待了五百位硅谷的企业家，而他不在被邀请之列。

他受了伤害，但仍去了 NeXT 上班。每天如此。

史蒂夫的最高价值并不在于他创造的东西有多新奇，而在于他创造的东西有多美好。

作为一个创新家，史蒂夫也有他自己的执着。如果他喜欢一件T恤，他能一下买十件一百件。在他帕罗奥尔托的家里面，黑色高领棉套衫，足够在场各位每人一件。

他不追求时髦，他觉得打扮应该符合自己的年纪。

他秉持的美学观点让我想起了一句话："时尚是现在的美丽和以后的丑陋；艺术是起初的丑陋和逐渐的美丽。"

史蒂夫始终渴望着能创造美丽。

他甚至希望被人误解。

尽管总统没有邀请他参加晚宴，但他却开着他的黑色跑车 —— 这是他买的第三辆或者第四辆一模一样的车 —— 去了 NeXT，他和他的团队正在秘密地开发一个平台，后来蒂姆·伯纳斯-李在这个平台之上开发出了万维网。

史蒂夫总是像女孩子一样，热衷于谈论关于爱的话题。爱，是他最出众的美德，是他的万神之神。对周围人的感情生活他亦是十分关心。

Laurene. "There's this beautiful woman and she's really smart and she has this dog and I'm going to marry her."

When Reed was born, he began gushing and never stopped. He was a physical dad, with each of his children. He fretted over Lisa's boyfriends and Erin's travel and skirt lengths and Eve's safety around the horses she adored.

None of us who attended Reed's graduation party will ever forget the scene of Reed and Steve slow dancing.

His abiding love for Laurene sustained him. He believed that love happened all the time, everywhere. In that most important way, Steve was never ironic, never cynical, never pessimistic. I try to learn from that, still.

Steve had been successful at a young age, and he felt that had isolated him. Most of the choices he made from the time I knew him were designed to dissolve the walls around him. A middle-class boy from Los Altos, he fell in love with a middle-class girl from New Jersey. It was important to both of them to raise Lisa, Reed, Erin and Eve as grounded, normal children. Their house didn't intimidate with art or polish; in fact, for many of the first years I knew Steve and Lo together, dinner was served on the grass, and sometimes consisted of just one vegetable. Lots of that one vegetable. But one. Broccoli. In season. Simply prepared. With just the right, recently snipped, herb.

Even as a young millionaire, Steve always picked me up at the airport. He'd be standing there in his jeans.

When a family member called him at work, his secretary Linetta answered, "Your dad's in a meeting.

每当他看到颇有魅力的男士时，他总会打电话给人家说："你还是单身吗？你愿意和我妹妹共进晚餐吗？"

我还记得那天，他初遇劳伦，然后打电话给她："有位美丽的女士，她聪明，她养狗，我想娶她。"

里德出生的时候，他一直在唠叨个不停。他是个很爱操心的老爸。他为丽莎的男朋友着急，为艾琳的旅行着急，以及她们裙子的长度，为爱马的伊芙的安全着急。

我们参加了里德的毕业典礼，史蒂夫和里德一起慢舞的情景永远留在我们记忆中。

他对劳伦恒久不渝的爱是他力量的源泉。他相信爱无处不在，无时不在，最重要的是，史蒂夫从不挖苦别人，从不愤世嫉俗，从不悲观厌世，这也是我一直在向他学习的地方。

史蒂夫年少有为，但成功也带给了他孤独。从我认识他起，他做的大部分决定都是为了化解周围那堵无形的"墙"。一个来自洛斯拉图斯中产阶级家庭的男孩，爱上了来自一个纽泽西中产阶级家庭的女孩。能让丽莎、里德、艾琳和伊芙四个孩子踏实健康的成长，对他们俩来说是至关重要的事情。他们的家没有华丽的装饰，实际上，就我所知，在婚后的很多年里，史蒂夫两口子是坐在草地上吃晚餐的，有时候只有一种蔬菜，比如西兰花，都是时令蔬菜，菜量很大，加上一点刚采摘下来的香料，简单烹制一下即可。

即使作为一个年轻的百万富翁，史蒂夫还是会亲自去

Would you like me to interrupt him?"

When Reed insisted on dressing up as a witch every Halloween, Steve, Laurene, Erin and Eve all went wiccan.

They once embarked on a kitchen remodel; it took years. They cooked on a hotplate in the garage. The Pixar building, under construction during the same period, finished in half the time. And that was it for the Palo Alto house. The bathrooms stayed old. But — and this was a crucial distinction — it had been a great house to start with; Steve saw to that.

This is not to say that he didn't enjoy his success: he enjoyed his success a lot, just minus a few zeros. He told me how much he loved going to the Palo Alto bike store and gleefully realizing he could afford to buy the best bike there.

And he did.

Steve was humble. Steve liked to keep learning.

Once, he told me if he'd grown up differently, he might have become a mathematician. He spoke reverently about colleges and loved walking around the Stanford campus. In the last year of his life, he studied a book of paintings by Mark Rothko, an artist he hadn't known about before, thinking of what could inspire people on the walls of a future Apple campus.

Steve cultivated whimsy. What other C.E.O. knows the history of English and Chinese tea roses and has a favorite David Austin rose?

He had surprises tucked in all his pockets. I'll venture that Laurene will discover treats — songs he loved, a

机场接我，他就站在那儿，穿着牛仔裤。

如果工作的时候，家人打电话找他，秘书琳内塔总会接起来说："你的爸爸在开会呢，需要我去打断他吗？"

每年的万圣节，里德都要打扮成女巫，于是史蒂夫、劳伦、艾琳和伊芙都会扮成巫师的模样。

他们曾经改造过一次厨房，却花了很多年的时间。于是他们只好把电炉放到车库里做饭。当时皮克斯的大楼正盖到一半，他们在帕罗奥尔托的房子就是这个样子的，浴室已经很旧了。但是 —— 这也是至关重要的一点 —— 却是个安乐窝，史蒂夫看重的就是这一点。

这并不是说，他不享受自己的成功：他也乐在其中，但却没有多大的欲望。他告诉我当他在帕罗奥尔托的自行车店里看到自己能买得起里面最贵的自行车时，真是心花怒放。

史蒂夫是个谦虚的人，他从没停止过学习。

有一次，他对我说，如果他的人生可以再来一次，他可能会成为一名数学家。每当说起大学，他的语气总是很恭敬，他喜欢在斯坦福的校园里散步。在他生命的最后几年，还在跟着马克·罗斯科的一本书学画画，他之前并不了解这位艺术家，但这本书却让他开始思考，如何利用苹果园区的墙壁来激发人们的灵感。

史蒂夫经常会有一些奇思怪想。除了他，还有哪个CEO了解茶香月季的中英文历史，并对大卫·奥斯丁玫瑰的津津乐道？

poem he cut out and put in a drawer — even after 20 years of an exceptionally close marriage. I spoke to him every other day or so, but when I opened The New York Times and saw a feature on the company's patents, I was still surprised and delighted to see a sketch for a perfect staircase.

With his four children, with his wife, with all of us, Steve had a lot of fun.

He treasured happiness.

Then, Steve became ill and we watched his life compress into a smaller circle. Once, he'd loved walking through Paris. He'd discovered a small handmade soba shop in Kyoto. He downhill skied gracefully. He cross-country skied clumsily. No more.

Eventually, even ordinary pleasures, like a good peach, no longer appealed to him.

Yet, what amazed me, and what I learned from his illness, was how much was still left after so much had been taken away.

I remember my brother learning to walk again, with a chair. After his liver transplant, once a day he would get up on legs that seemed too thin to bear him, arms pitched to the chair back. He'd push that chair down the Memphis hospital corridor towards the nursing station and then he'd sit down on the chair, rest, turn around and walk back again. He counted his steps and, each day, pressed a little farther.

Laurene got down on her knees and looked into his eyes.

"You can do this, Steve," she said. His eyes widened.

他的口袋里常常会装着一些稀奇古怪的东西。我觉得就算他和劳伦已经恩爱的过了二十年，劳伦也一定会发现他的这些宝贝 —— 他喜欢的歌曲、诗歌的片段，他都会放在一个抽屉里。我几乎每天都要和史蒂夫聊天，但当我翻开《纽约时报》，看到对他的公司专利产品的专题介绍的时候，仍然会为他们对某个楼梯的完美的草图设计而感到惊喜。

和他的四个孩子在一起，和他的妻子在一起，和我们大家在一起，史蒂夫感到无比快乐。

他把幸福视如珍宝。

史蒂夫生病之后，生活圈子陡然变小了。他曾经一度喜欢徒步穿越整个巴黎市。他曾经在京都发现了一家小小的手工荞麦面店。他曾经以优雅的姿势从山上滑雪而下，但对越野滑雪却不在行。而在他生病之后，这一切都一去无返。

到了最后，即使那些最平凡的快乐，比如一个美味的桃子，也无法再吸引他了。

在他生病之后，尽管失去了很多，但仍然有被他保留下来的品质，这些让人感到惊奇，我也从中受益匪浅。

我还记得哥哥再次拿着一把椅子学习走路的情景。做了肝移植手术之后，他的双腿变得非常瘦弱，难以支撑他站起来，他会扶着椅背，推着椅子沿着孟菲斯医院的走廊，走到护士站，然后在椅子上坐着休息一会儿，再原路返回。每天，他都会数着这次一共走了多少步，争取下次再走

His lips pressed into each other.

He tried. He always, always tried, and always with love at the core of that effort. He was an intensely emotional man.

I realized during that terrifying time that Steve was not enduring the pain for himself. He set destinations: his son Reed's graduation from high school, his daughter Erin's trip to Kyoto, the launching of a boat he was building on which he planned to take his family around the world and where he hoped he and Laurene would someday retire.

Even ill, his taste, his discrimination and his judgment held. He went through 67 nurses before finding kindred spirits and then he completely trusted the three who stayed with him to the end. Tracy. Arturo. Elham.

One time when Steve had contracted a tenacious pneumonia his doctor forbid everything — even ice. We were in a standard I.C.U. unit. Steve, who generally disliked cutting in line or dropping his own name, confessed that this once, he'd like to be treated a little specially.

I told him: Steve, this is special treatment.

He leaned over to me, and said: "I want it to be a little more special."

Intubated, when he couldn't talk, he asked for a notepad. He sketched devices to hold an iPad in a hospital bed. He designed new fluid monitors and x-ray equipment. He redrew that not-quite-special-enough hospital unit. And every time his wife walked into the

远一点。

劳伦曾经跪在他前面，看着他的眼睛，说："史蒂夫，你可以做到的。"

他睁大眼睛，双唇紧闭。

他努力了，他一直、一直在努力，他一直在爱的陪伴下在努力着。他是个如此感情丰富的男人。

我知道，在那段难熬的日子里，史蒂夫承受这些痛苦并不是为了他自己。他给自己定了目标：要等到儿子里德大学毕业，要等到女儿艾琳从京都旅行回来，要等到他打造的那条船下水——等到他和劳伦有一天退休了，他要开着它带着全家人周游世界。

病魔没有影响他的品位、洞察力和判断。他换了六十七个护士才终于找到和他志趣相投的护士，而且给予他们完全的信任，这三个人一直陪他走完人生的最后一程人——特雷西、爱徒罗和伊尔哈姆。

有一次，史蒂夫患上了肺炎，久治不愈，他的医生禁止他吃包括冰块在内的很多东西。我们进入了标准重症监护室。史蒂夫一向不喜欢插队，不喜欢用自己的名字搞特权，但这一次，他承认获得一点特别优待还挺好的。

我告诉他：史蒂夫，这已经是特别优待了。

他弯下腰对我说："我想要可以再特别一点。"

插管治疗的时候，他无法说话，于是找人要了一个笔记本。原来，他画了一张在病床上可以支撑iPad设备的草图，除此之外，他还设计了一个全新的透析液监视器、一

21

room, I watched his smile remake itself on his face.

For the really big, big things, you have to trust me, he wrote on his sketchpad. He looked up. You have to.

By that, he meant that we should disobey the doctors and give him a piece of ice.

None of us knows for certain how long we'll be here. On Steve's better days, even in the last year, he embarked upon projects and elicited promises from his friends at Apple to finish them. Some boat builders in the Netherlands have a gorgeous stainless steel hull ready to be covered with the finishing wood. His three daughters remain unmarried, his two youngest still girls, and he'd wanted to walk them down the aisle as he'd walked me the day of my wedding.

We all — in the end — die in medias res. In the middle of a story. Of many stories.

I suppose it's not quite accurate to call the death of someone who lived with cancer for years unexpected, but Steve's death was unexpected for us.

What I learned from my brother's death was that character is essential: What he was, was how he died.

Tuesday morning, he called me to ask me to hurry up to Palo Alto. His tone was affectionate, dear, loving, but like someone whose luggage was already strapped onto the vehicle, who was already on the beginning of his journey, even as he was sorry, truly deeply sorry, to be leaving us.

He started his farewell and I stopped him. I said, "Wait. I'm coming. I'm in a taxi to the airport. I'll be there."

"I'm telling you now because I'm afraid you won't

台X光设备，甚至把现在他住的这个不够特别的病房重新设计了一下。每当他妻子走进来，他脸上总会绽放笑容。

还有一些他觉得非常重要的事情，他也会写在本子上，然后抬头看着我。

他写的是，他想让我们背着医生不知道，给他吃一块冰。

没人知道我们还要在那个病房里待多久。即使是在他生命的最后几年，只要病情稍好一点，他就会着手进行一些项目，还向苹果的同事们保证说一定能做完。那时，荷兰的造船师已经把船的不锈钢外壳打造好完成，非常漂亮，就差在外壳上覆盖上木材了。他的三个女儿都还没有结婚，最小的两个甚至还没有成年，他希望有一天能陪着他们走完教堂的红毯，如同他在我的婚礼上面陪我走过的那样。

我们都会面对死亡，只是谁比谁先走而已。

我知道，对于一个罹患癌症多年的人来说，他的去世不应该是意料之外的事情，但史蒂夫的离去对我们来说确实是始料未及的。

哥哥的离开，让我明白了性格的重要：他是什么样的人，就会以什么样的方式死去。

那个星期二早晨，他打电话给我，要我赶紧赶到帕罗奥尔托，语气温柔而深情，就像一个已经把行李装车，即将踏上一段新的旅程的人，即使他有万分不舍和歉意，仍然不得不离去。

make it on time, honey."

When I arrived, he and his Laurene were joking together like partners who'd lived and worked together every day of their lives. He looked into his children's eyes as if he couldn't unlock his gaze.

Until about 2 in the afternoon, his wife could rouse him, to talk to his friends from Apple.

Then, after awhile, it was clear that he would no longer wake to us.

His breathing changed. It became severe, deliberate, purposeful. I could feel him counting his steps again, pushing farther than before.

This is what I learned: he was working at this, too. Death didn't happen to Steve, he achieved it.

He told me, when he was saying goodbye and telling me he was sorry, so sorry we wouldn't be able to be old together as we'd always planned, that he was going to a better place.

Dr. Fischer gave him a 50/50 chance of making it through the night.

He made it through the night, Laurene next to him on the bed sometimes jerked up when there was a longer pause between his breaths. She and I looked at each other, then he would heave a deep breath and begin again.

This had to be done. Even now, he had a stern, still handsome profile, the profile of an absolutist, a romantic. His breath indicated an arduous journey, some steep path, altitude.

He seemed to be climbing.

他在电话里开始和我道别，我阻止了他，我说："等着我，我这就出发，打车去机场，我马上到。"

"亲爱的，我现在就想对你说，我害怕时间来不及了。"

当我赶到的时候，看到他和劳伦正在相互开着玩笑，就像一对每天生活工作在一起的搭档一样。然后，他看着孩子们的眼睛，凝视许久。

下午两点，他的妻子还能够把他唤醒，让他和苹果的朋友们说说话。

片刻之后，他已经无法再为我们而醒来了。

他用尽最后一丝力气努力呼吸，尽管是那样艰难。我能感到他又在一步一步数着他的脚步，想能走能更远一点、更远一点。

我突然明白了：这对他来说，亦是一种工作。死亡不会发生在史蒂夫身上，他做到了。

他对我说，他和我道别，他很抱歉，抱歉我们不能像原来说好的那样一起慢慢变老，他现在有更好的地方要去。

费舍尔医生说，他坚持活过当晚的机会只有一半。

他挺过了那晚。劳伦睡在他旁边的床上，一听到他的呼吸停顿时间久了，就会马上惊醒，和我对视一下，直到他又深呼吸一下，恢复正常。

他要自己必须做到。直到现在，他留给我们的仍然是严肃、淡定、英俊的形象，专制而浪漫。他的呼吸表明了这趟旅程的艰辛不易，道路崎岖不平，如同攀登山峰。

但凭借着这种信念、工作热情和精神力量，亲爱的史

But with that will, that work ethic, that strength, there was also sweet Steve's capacity for wonderment, the artist's belief in the ideal, the still more beautiful later.

Steve's final words, hours earlier, were monosyllables, repeated three times.

Before embarking, he'd looked at his sister Patty, then for a long time at his children, then at his life's partner, Laurene, and then over their shoulders past them.

Steve's final words were:

OH WOW. OH WOW. OH WOW.

蒂夫对新奇事物的包容力、对理想艺术家般的信念，将会在未来的日子里变得越来越动人。

史蒂夫在去世前的几个小时里，说了最后的话，都是一些单音节词，一共重复了三遍。

去世之前，他看看他的妹妹帕蒂，看了很久孩子们，然后又看了他的人生伴侣劳伦，最后把目光望向远方。

说出了最后几个字："OH WOW.OH WOW. OH WOW."

1. 童年

Childhood

| 童年的乔布斯　　　　　| Steve jobs 'childhood

1972年,乔布斯在高中年
鉴上的照片

Jobs' photo in High
school yearbook,1972

It started before I was born. My biological mother was a young, unwed college graduate student, and she decided to put me up for adoption. She felt very strongly that I should be adopted by college graduates, so everything was all set for me to be adopted at birth by a lawyer and his wife. Except that when I popped out they decided at the last minute that they really wanted a girl. So my parents, who were on a waiting list, got a call in the middle of the night asking: "We have an unexpected baby boy; do you want him?" They said: "Of course." My biological mother later found out that my mother had never graduated from college and that my father had never graduated from high school. She refused to sign the final adoption papers. She only relented a few months later when my parents promised that I would someday go to college.

Stanford commencement speech, June 2005

"So does that mean your real parents didn't want you?" the girl asked. Lightning bolts went off in my head, I remember running into the house, crying. And my parents said, "No, you have to understand. " They were very serious and looked me straight in the eye. They said, "We specifically picked you out. " Both of my parents said that and repeated it slowly for me. And they put an emphasis on every word in that sentence.

Steve Jobs, By Walter Isaacson, 2011

故事从我出生的时候讲起。我的亲生母亲是一个年轻的、没有结婚的大学毕业生。她决定让别人收养我，她十分想让我被大学毕业生收养。所以在我出生的时候，她已经做好了一切的准备工作，能使得我被一个律师和他的妻子所收养。但是她没有料到，当我出生之后，律师夫妇突然决定他们想要一个女孩。 所以我的养父母（他们还在我亲生父母的观察名单上）突然在半夜接到了一个电话："我们现在这儿有一个不小心生出来的男婴，你们想要他吗？"他们回答道："当然！"但是我亲生母亲随后发现，我的养母从来没有上过大学，我的父亲甚至从没有读过高中。她拒绝签这个收养合同。只是在几个月以后，我的父母答应她一定要让我上大学，那个时候她才同意。

（当我告诉一个女孩我是被领养时）"这是不是说明你的亲生父母不要你了？"女孩问。天哪，我当时就像被闪电击中了一样，我跑回家，大声哭喊。我父母说："不是这样的，你要理解这件事情。"他们当时很严肃，直直地看着我的眼睛。他们说："我们是专门挑的你。"他们两人都这么说，并且放慢语速向我重复这句话。他们强调了这句话里的每一个字。

斯坦福毕业典礼演讲，2005年6月

《史蒂夫·乔布斯传》，沃尔特·艾萨克森著，2011年

My dad did not have a deep understanding of electronics, but he'd encountered it a lot in automobiles and other things he would fix. He showed me the rudiments of electronics, and I got very interested in that.

Steve Jobs,
By Walter Isaacason, 2011

I had a great childhood. I turned out okay.

Steve Jobs,
By Walter Isaacason, 2011

"I was kind of bored for the first few years, so I occupied myself by getting into trouble.

Steve Jobs,
By Walter Isaacson, 2011

I saw my first desktop computer there. It was called the 9100A, and it was a glorified calculator but also really the first desktop computer. It was huge, maybe forty pounds, but it was a beauty of a thing. I fell in love with it.

Steve Jobs,
By Walter Isaacson, 2011

When I was 13, I think, I called up...Hewlett and Packard were my idols. And I called up Bill Hewlett, cause he lived in Palo Alto, and there were no unlisted numbers in the phone book...And he picked up the phone and I talked to him and I asked him if he'd give me some spare parts for something I was building called a frequency counter. And he did, but in addition to that he gave me something way more important. He gave me a job that summer. A summer job at Hewlett-Packard, right here (on) in Santa Clara, off 280, the division that built frequency counters. And I was in heaven.

Steve Jobs' last public speech in the meeting of Cupertino City in 2011

我的父亲对电子设备并没有很深的了解，但他经常在汽车以及其他修理对象上跟电子设备打交道。他为我展示了电子设备的基本原理，我觉得很有趣。

《史蒂夫·乔布斯传》，沃尔特·艾萨克森著，2011 年

我的童年很棒，我好好地长大了。

《史蒂夫·乔布斯传》，沃尔特·艾萨克森著，2011 年

在学校的最初几年我觉得很无聊，所以我就不断惹麻烦。

《史蒂夫·乔布斯传》，沃尔特·艾萨克森著，2011 年

我在那里（惠普实验室）第一次见到了台式计算机，它被称为 9100A，是一台被神化了的计算器，但也确实是第一台台式计算机。它身形巨大，大概有 40 磅重，但它真的很美，我爱上了它。

《史蒂夫·乔布斯传》，沃尔特·艾萨克森著，2011 年

打小我就是惠普创始人休利特和帕尔德的粉丝。休利特住在帕洛阿尔托，13 岁那年我给他打了个电话，那时候所有的电话号码都印在电话本里了……他接起电话，我问他是否能送我些零件做频率计数器。他不仅答应了，还给了我一份工作，惠普的暑期短工，就在圣克拉拉 280 号公路旁边，我被分在计频器部门，简直像去了天堂。

乔布斯在库比蒂诺市议会最后的公开演讲，2011 年

When I was young, there was an amazing publication called The Whole Earth Catalog, which was one of the bibles of my generation. It was created by a fellow named Stewart Brand not far from here in Menlo Park, and he brought it to life with his poetic touch. This was in the late 1960's, before personal computers and desktop publishing, so it was all made with typewriters, scissors, and polaroid cameras. It was sort of like Google in paperback form, 35 years before Google came along: it was idealistic, and overflowing with neat tools and great notions.

Stanford commencement speech, June 2005

Stewart and his team put out several issues of The Whole Earth Catalog, and then when it had run its course, they put out a final issue. It was the mid-1970s, and I was your age. On the back cover of their final issue was a photograph of an early morning country road, the kind you might find yourself hitchhiking on if you were so adventurous. Beneath it were the words: "Stay Hungry. Stay Foolish." It was their farewell message as they signed off.

Stanford commencement speech, June 2005

我年轻的时候，有一本叫做《全球概览》的振聋发聩的杂志，它是我们那一代人的圣经之一。它是一个叫斯图尔特·布兰德的家伙在离这里不远的洛帕克市编写的，他像诗一般神奇地将这本书带到了这个世界。那是六十年代后期，在个人电脑出现之前，所以这本书全部是用打字机、剪刀还有偏光镜制造的。有点像用软皮包装的谷歌，却比谷歌早出现35年。这份刊物是理想主义的，其中有许多灵巧的工具和伟大的想法。

斯坦福毕业典礼演讲，2005年6月

斯图尔特和他的伙伴出版了几期《全球概览》，当它完成了自己使命的时候，他们做出了最后一期的目录。那是在（上世纪）七十年代的中期，你们的时代。在最后一期的封底上是清晨乡村公路的照片（如果你有冒险精神的话，你可以自己找到这条路的），在照片之下有这样一段话："求知若饥，虚心若愚。"这是他们停刊的告别语。

斯坦福毕业典礼演讲，2005年6月

One of my role models is Bob Dylan. As I grew up, I learned the lyrics to all his songs and watched him never stand still. If you look at the artists, if they get really good, it always OCCURS to them at some point that they can do this one thing for the rest of their lives, and they can be really successful to the outside world but not really be successful to themselves. That's the moment that an artist really decides who he or she is. If they keep on risking failure, they're still artists. Dylan and Pica-SSO were always risking failure.

CNNMoney / *Fortune,*
November 9, 1998

I got stoned for the first time that summer. I was fifteen, and then began using pot regularly

Steve Jobs,
By Walter Isaacson, 2011

I came of age at a magical time, Our consciousness was raised by Zen, and also by LSD." Even later in life he would credit psychedelic drugs for making him more enlightened. "Taking LSD was a profound experience, one of the most important things in my life. LSD shows you that there's another side to the coin, and you can't remember it when it wears off, but you know it. It reinforced my sense of what was important—creating great things instead of making money, putting things back into the stream of history and of human consciousness as much as I could.

Steve Jobs,
By Walter Isaacson, 2011

鲍勃·迪伦是我的榜样之一。我年少时就把他每首歌的歌词记得滚瓜烂熟，而且发现他永远都在进步。如果你留意观察那些真正优秀的艺术家，你会发现，他们常常在某个时候愿意为了某一件事情穷其余生的精力，对于外界来说，他们很成功；但在他们自己看来，却并非如此 —— 特别时当他们真的决定要做某事的时候。如果他们继续冒着失败的风险做下去，他们仍然是艺术家 —— 迪伦和毕加索就是如此。

美国有线电视新闻网财经频道/《财富》杂志，1998年9月9日

15岁时的夏天，我第一次抽大麻，之后就经常抽了。

《史蒂夫·乔布斯传》，沃尔特·艾萨克森著，2011年

我当时身处一个神奇的时代，提升我们觉悟的是禅宗，还有迷幻药。使用迷幻药是一段意义非凡的经历，也是我一生中最重要的事情之一。迷幻药让你看到硬币的另一面，当药效退去之后你就记不清楚了，但你知道有这么一回事。它让我更清楚什么是重要的 —— 创造伟大的发明，而不是赚钱。应该尽我所能，将此生放回历史和人类思想的长河。

《史蒂夫·乔布斯传》，沃尔特·艾萨克森著，2011年

When I was 17, I read a quote that went something like: "If you live each day as if it was your last, someday you'll most certainly be right. " It made an impression on me, and since then, for the past 33 years, I have looked in the mirror every morning and asked myself: "If today were the last day of my life, would I want to do what I am about to do today?" And whenever the answer has been "No" for too many days in a row, I know I need to change something.

Stanford commencement speech, June 2005

The kids who went to Stanford, they already knew what they wanted to do, They weren't really artistic. I wanted something that was more artistic and interesting.

Steve Jobs, By Walter Isaacson, 2011

我十七岁的时候，读到了一句话："如果你把每一天都当作生命中最后一天去生活的话，那么有一天你会发现你是正确的。"这句话给我留下了深刻的印象。从那时开始，过了33年，我在每天早晨都会对着镜子问自己："如果今天是我生命中的最后一天，你会不会完成你今天想做的事情呢？"当答案连续很多次被给予"不是"的时候，我知道自己需要改变某些事情了。

斯坦福毕业典礼演讲，2005年6月

去念斯坦福的人，他们已经知道自己想要什么了，他们一点儿艺术性都没有。我想要上的是更富有艺术性的、更有趣的学校。

《史蒂夫·乔布斯传》，沃尔特·艾萨克森著，2011年

And 17 years later I did go to college. But I naively chose a college that was almost as expensive as Stanford, and all of my working-class parents' savings were being spent on my college tuition. After six months, I couldn't see the value in it. I had no idea what I wanted to do with my life and no idea how college was going to help me figure it out. And here I was spending all of the money my parents had saved their entire life. So I decided to drop out and trust that it would all work out OK. It was pretty scary at the time, but looking back it was one of the best decisions I ever made. The minute I dropped out I could stop taking the required classes that didn't interest me, and begin dropping in on the ones that looked interesting.

Stanford commencement speech, June 2005

It wasn't all romantic. I didn't have a dorm room, so I slept on the floor in friends' rooms, I returned coke bottles for the 5¢ deposits to buy food with, and I would walk the 7 miles across town every Sunday night to get one good meal a week at the Hare Krishna temple. I loved it. And much of what I stumbled into by following my curiosity and intuition turned out to be priceless later on.

Stanford commencement speech, June 2005

十七岁那年，我真的上了大学。但是我很愚蠢地选择了一个几乎和你们斯坦福大学一样贵的学校，我父母还处于蓝领阶层，他们几乎把所有积蓄都花在了我的学费上面。在六个月后，我已经看不到其中的价值所在。我不知道我想要在生命中做什么，我也不知道大学能帮助我找到怎样的答案。但是在这里，我几乎花光了我父母这一辈子的所有积蓄。所以我决定要退学，我觉得这是个正确的决定。不能否认，我当时确实非常的害怕，但是现在回头看看，那的确是我这一生中最棒的一个决定。在我做出退学决定的那一刻，我终于可以不必去读那些令我提不起丝毫兴趣的课程了。然后我还可以去修那些看起来有点意思的课程。

斯坦福毕业典礼演讲，2005年6月

但是这并不是那么浪漫。我失去了我的宿舍，所以我只能在朋友房间的地板上面睡觉，我去捡5美分的可乐瓶子，仅仅为了填饱肚子，在星期天的晚上，我需要走七英里的路程，穿过这个城市到Hare Krishna寺庙，只是为了能吃上饭 —— 这个星期唯一一顿好一点的饭。但是我喜欢这样。我跟着我的直觉和好奇心走，遇到的很多东西，此后被证明是无价之宝。

斯坦福毕业典礼演讲，2005年6月

Reed College at that time offered perhaps the best calligraphy instruction in the country. Throughout the campus every poster, every label on every drawer, was beautifully hand calligraphed. Because I had dropped out and didn't have to take the normal classes, I decided to take a calligraphy class to learn how to do this. I learned about serif and san serif typefaces, about varying the amount of space between different letter combinations, about what makes great typography great. It was beautiful, historical, artistically subtle in a way that science can't capture, and I found it fascinating.

Stanford commencement speech, June 2005

None of this had even a hope of any practical application in my life. But ten years later, when we were designing the first Macintosh computer, it all came back to me. And we designed it all into the Mac. It was the first computer with beautiful typography. If I had never dropped in on that single course in college, the Mac would have never had multiple typefaces or proportionally spaced fonts. And since Windows just copied the Mac, its likely that no personal computer would have them. If I had never dropped out, I would have never dropped in on this calligraphy class, and personal computers might not have the wonderful typography that they do. Of course it was impossible to connect the dots looking forward when I was in college. But it was very, very clear looking backwards ten years later.

Stanford commencement speech, June 2005

里德学院在那时提供也许是整个美国最好的美术字课程。在这个大学里面的每个海报，每个抽屉的标签上面全都是漂亮的美术字。因为我退学了，没有受到正规的训练，所以我决定去参加这个课程，去学学怎样写出漂亮的美术字。我学到了san serif 和serif字体，我学会了怎么样在不同的字母组合之中改变空格的长度，还有怎么样才能作出最棒的印刷式样。那是一种科学永远不能捕捉到的、美丽的、真实的艺术精妙，我发现那实在是太美妙了。

斯坦福毕业典礼演讲，2005 年 6 月

当时看起来这些东西在我的生命中，好像都没有什么实际应用的可能。但是十年之后，当我们在设计第一台Macintosh电脑的时候，就不是那样了。我把当时我学的那些家伙全都设计进了Mac。那是第一台使用了漂亮的印刷字体的电脑。如果我当时没有退学，就不会有机会去参加这个我感兴趣的美术字课程，Mac就不会有这么多丰富的字体，以及赏心悦目的字体间距。那么现在个人电脑就不会有现在这么美妙的字型了。当然我在大学的时候，还不可能把从前的点点滴滴串连起来，但是当我十年后回顾这一切的时候，真的豁然开朗了。

斯坦福毕业典礼演讲，2005 年 6 月

Western rational thought is not an innate human characteristic; it is learned and is the great achievement of Western civilization. In the villages of India, they never learned it. They learned something else, which is in some ways just as valuable but in other ways is not. That's the power of intuition and experiential wisdom.

Steve Jobs,
By Walter Isaacson, 2011

Coming back after seven months in Indian villages, I saw the craziness of the Western world as well as its capacity for rational thought. If you just sit and observe, you will see how restless your mind is. If you try to calm it, it only makes it worse, but over time it does calm, and when it does, there's room to hear more subtle things—that's when your intuition starts to blossom and you start to see things more clearly and be in the present more. Your mind just slows down, and you see a tremendous expanse in the moment. You see so much more than you could see before. It's a discipline; you have to practice it.

Steve Jobs,
By Walter Isaacson, 2011

There's a phrase in Buddhism, 'Beginner's mind.' it's wonderful to have a beginner's mind.

*Wired,*1996

西方的理性思维并不是人类先天就具有的，而是通过学习获得的，它是西方文明的一项伟大成就。而在印度的村子里，人们从未学习过理性思维。他们学习的是其他东西，在某些方面与理性思维同样有价值，那就是直观和经验智慧的力量。

《史蒂夫·乔布斯传》，沃尔特·艾萨克森著，2011 年

在印度的村庄待了 7 个月后再回到美国，我看到了西方世界的疯狂以及理性思维的局限。如果你坐下来静静观察，你会发现自己的心灵有多焦躁。如果你想平静下来，那情况只会更糟，但是时间久了之后总会平静下来，心里就会有空间让你聆听更加微妙的东西——这时候你的直觉就开始发展，你看事情会更加透彻，也更能感受现实的环境。你的心灵逐渐平静下来，你的视界会极大地延伸。你能看到之前看不到的东西。这是一种修行，你必须不断练习。

《史蒂夫·乔布斯传》，沃尔特·艾萨克森著，2011 年

佛教中有一句话：初学者的心态，拥有初学者的心态是一件了不起的事情。

《连线》杂志，1996 年

2. 创业
Start

1977年4月，乔布斯和他的苹果电脑参加展销会

Jobs and his Apple Computer attend the exhibition, April,1977

1976年4月1日，史蒂夫·乔布斯、史蒂夫·沃兹尼克以及罗纳德·维尼签署了一份合同，成立了苹果公司

April 1, 1976, The Apple Inc. founding partnership agreement was signed by Steve Wozniak, Steve Jobs and Ronald Wayne

I was lucky – I found what I loved to do early in life. Woz and I started Apple in my parents garage when I was 20.

Stanford Commencement Speech, June2005

My vision was to create the first fully packaged computer, We were no longer aiming for the handful of hobbyists who liked to assemble their own computers, who knew how to buy transformers and keyboards. For every one of them there were a thousand people who would want the machine to be ready to run.

Steve Jobs,
By Walter Isaacson, 2011

I had just come back from the apple farm. It sounded fun, spirited, and not intimidating. Apple took the edge off the word 'computer.' Plus, it would get us ahead of Atari in the phone book.

Steve Jobs,
By Walter Isaacson, 2011

It looks a bunch of rambunctious upstarts, working with very little resources but a certain vision and commitment, to do it.

Newsweek,1985

We were joined by Mike Markkula and soon after that our first president, Mike Scott.

The Launch of iMac, May 6, 1998

我非常幸运，因为我在很早的时候就找到了我钟爱的东西。沃兹和我在二十岁的时候就在父母的车库里面开创了苹果公司。

斯坦福毕业典礼演讲，2005年6月

"我的想法是制造第一台整合所有部件的电脑，"我回忆道，"我们的目标客户不再是少数喜欢自己组装电脑、知道如何购买变压器和键盘的业余爱好者。希望电脑拿到手就可以运行的人，其数量是业余爱好者的1000倍。"

《史蒂夫·乔布斯传》，沃尔特·艾萨克森著，2011年

（关于公司的名字的由来）我刚刚从一个苹果农场回来想到的。（苹果）这名字听上去有意思，有活力，不吓人。"苹果"削弱了"电脑"这个词的锐气。还有，这能让我们在电话簿上排在雅达利之前。

《史蒂夫·乔布斯传》，沃尔特·艾萨克森著，2011年

公司起步时，我带领一群狂乱且毫无纪律观念的自命不凡之辈开始创业。我们当时可利用的资源真是少得可怜，但我们都有一种创见性和为事业献身的精神。

《商业周刊》，1985年

后来，麦克·马库拉加入了我们。不久之后，我们还迎来了我们的第一任总裁，麦克·斯科特。

iMac发布会，1985年5月6日

Did Alexander Graham Bell do any market research before he invented the telephone?

Popular Science, 1984

If we can rap about their needs, feelings and motivations, we can respond appropriately by giving them what they want.

Interface, July 1976

In 1977 Apple, a young fledgling company on the West Coast, invents the Apple II, the first personal computer.

Steve Jobs speech on IBM in 1983

It was clear to me that for every hardware hobbyist who wanted to assemble his own computer,there were a thousand people who couldn't do that but wanted to mess around with programming…just like I did when I was 10. My dream for the Apple II was to sell the first real packaged computer…I got a bug up my rear that I wanted the computer in a plastic case.

Apple Design, 1997

When we first designed the Apple II in a garage, and we thought if we ever built 50 a month, we would be doing great.

Steve Jobs speech in Apple's 1984 annual shareholder's meeting

亚历山大·格雷厄姆·贝尔在发明电话前做过任何市场调研吗？

《大众科学》，1984 年

（在产品设计上方面）如果我可以了解他们（顾客）的需求、感受和动机，我们就可以做出正确的回应，生产出他们所需要的产品。

《界面》，1976 年 7 月

1977 年，苹果作为西海岸的一家新兴公司，发明了 Apple Ⅱ，按照今天的定义，即第一台个人电脑。

史蒂夫·乔布斯针对 IBM 的演讲，1983 年

每一个硬件迷都希望能够自己组装电脑，他们里面有很多人虽然还做不到这个，但也想自己搞搞编程……我十岁的时候也做过这个。我希望能在 Apple Ⅱ 上实现我的一个梦想，那就是出售真正的全套电脑……我还希望能把电脑的机箱做成塑料的。

《苹果的设计》，1997 年

我们最初是在车库里设计的 Apple Ⅱ，大多数人并不知道我们最初的想法就是在车库里生产。我们想，如果我们能每个月生产 50 台，我们就做得很好了。

乔布斯在苹果股东大会上的演讲，1984 年

When we first started Apple we really built the first computer because we wanted one. We designed this crazy new computer with color and a whole bunch of other things called the Apple II which you have probably heard about. We had a passion to do this one simple thing which was to get a bunch of computers to our friends SO they could have as much fun with them as we were.

Return to the Little Kingdom,2009

I sort of look at us as two of the luckiest guys on the planet because we found what we loved to do and we were at the right place at the right time. And so it's hard to be happier than that.

Steve Jobs and Bill Gates Interviews, May 30, 2007

I read something Bill Gates said about six months ago. He said, "I worked really,really hard in my twenties. "And I know what he means. because I worked really,really hard in my twenties. too-seven days a week, lots of hours every day. But you can't do it forever. You don't want to do it forever.

Time. October 10,1999

我们最开始成立苹果公司，制造出一台真正的电脑的原因，就是因为我们自己想要一台电脑。我们设计的这个电脑很了不起，不仅有颜色，而且还有一大堆别的东西，我们叫它Apple II—— 你也可能听说过这个名字。我们热衷于做这件简单的事情，可以让朋友们都拥有电脑，让他们感受到和我们一样的乐趣。

《重返小王国》，2009 年

我们两个（乔布斯和比尔·盖茨）都是世界上最幸运的人，在正确的时间、正确的地点，找到了真正喜爱的事业。还有什么比这更棒的呢？

乔布斯和比尔·盖茨访谈，2007 年 5 月 30 日

大约半年前，我看了一些比尔·盖茨的演讲。他说："在我二十几岁的时候，我真的真的很努力地工作。"我知道他所指的是什么意思，因为我在我二十几岁的时候也很努力工作。一周连续七天，每天的大部分时间都扑在工作上。但你不能永远这样做，你也不想永远这样做下去。

《时代》杂志，1999 年 10 月 10 日

3. 发展

Development

1984年1月24日，时任
苹果董事会主席的乔布斯
在股东大会召开前夕倚着
麦金托什，和媒体聊天

January 24, 1984 Steve Jobs, Apple Chairman of the
Board, the eve of the general meeting of shareholders
held is leaning against Macintosh, chatting with media.

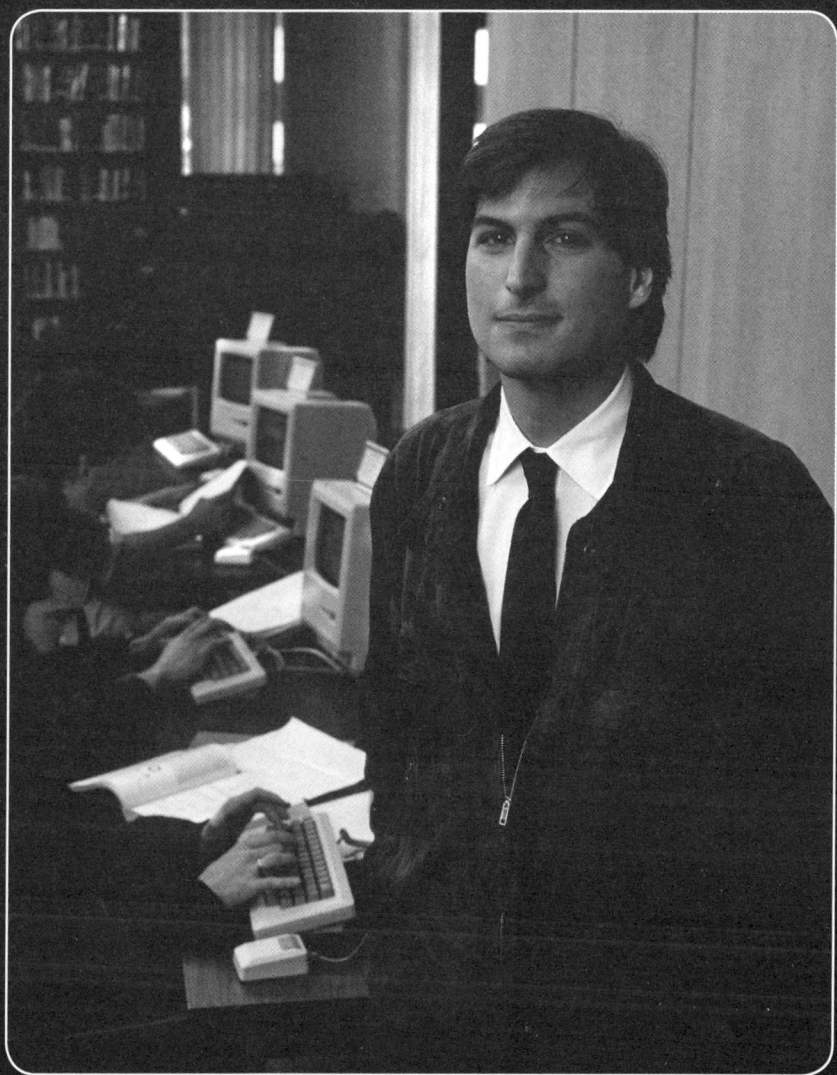

1984年乔布斯站在斯坦福大学图书馆内，身后是他开发的麦金塔电脑

Steve Jobs stands in front of a table full of Macintosh computers at Stanford University, 1984

I've got to learn to keep my feelings private.

Time, February 1982

The early 80's, 81. Apple II has become the world's most popular computer and Apple has grown to a three hundred million dollar company, becoming the fastest growing corporation in American business history.

Steve Jobs speech on IBM in 1983

It's more fun to be a pirate than to join the navy.

1982, quoted in *Odyssey*: Pepsi to Apple, 1987

The current wave of industrial design is Sony's high-tech look, which is gunmetal gray, maybe paint it black, do weird stuff to it, It's easy to do that. But it's not great. What we're going to do is make the products high-tech, and we're going to package them cleanly so that you know they're high-tech. We will fit them in a small package, and then we can make them beautiful and white, just like Braun does with its electronics.

Aspen design conference, 1983

So that's our approach. Very simple, and we're really shooting for Museum of Modern Art quality. The way we're running the company, the product design, the advertising, it all comes down to this: Let's make it simple. Really simple.

Aspen design conference, 1983

Simplicity is the ultimate sophistication.

Apple's first brochure

我得学会如何控制自己的情绪。

《时代》，1982年2月

80年代初，1981年，Apple II已成为世界上最流行的电脑，苹果公司也成长为一家拥有三亿美元资产的公司，是美国商业史上发展速度最快的公司。

史蒂夫·乔布斯针对IBM的演讲，1983年

成为海盗比加入海军更有意思。

《冒险历程：从百事到苹果》，1987年，引用乔布斯在1982年的话。

当下工业设计的潮流就是索尼的那种高科技感，也就是金属灰色，要么就涂成黑色，加一些怪异的设计。这么做很容易，但不够好，我们要做的，就是让产品科技感十足，然后用上简单干净的包装，让科技感一目了然。我们会把产品放在小包装盒里，让它们看上去纯白漂亮，就像博朗生产的电器一样。

阿斯彭设计大会，1983年

我们的设计思想就是：极致的简约，我们追求的是能让产品达到在任何现代艺术博物馆展出的品质。我们管理公司、设计产品、广告宣传的理念就是一句话：让我们做的简单一点，真正的简单。

阿斯彭设计大会，1983年

至繁归于至简。

苹果第一版宣传册

63

It's Not Done Until It Ships.

Folklore. org,January 1983

The journey is the reward

Folklore. org,January 1983

Empathy, focus,impute.

The Apple Marketing Philosophy, 1977

Apple is the 21 st century bike.

the Wall Street journal, 1980

The people who are doing the work are the moving force behind the Macintosh. My job is to create a space for them, to clear out the rest of the organization and keep it at bay.

Macworld , 1984

My job is not to be easy on people. My job is to take these great people we have and to push them and make them even better.

Macworld , 1984

Actually,making an insanely great product has a lot to do with the process of making the product, how you learn things and adopt new ideas and throw out old ideas.

Playboy,February 1985

产品上市工作才算完成。

Folklore.org
1983 年 1 月

过程是一种奖励。

Folklore.org
1983 年 1 月

（我们的营销哲学）
共鸣，专注，灌输。

苹果营销哲学, 1977 年

苹果电脑就是21世纪人类的自行车。

《华尔街日报》, 1980 年

推动麦金塔电脑前进的就是这些有创意的工作人员。我要做的就是为他们创造空间，清除障碍，将不利因素挡在外面。

Macworld, 1984 年

我的工作不是做老好人，而是领导我手下的这些人才，并不断鞭策他们，让他们做得更好。

Macworld, 1984 年

实际上，要想做出一个酷毙了的产品，制造的过程很重要 —— 你要如何学习，如何采用新的想法，如何摒弃旧的观念。

《花花公子》杂志，
1985 年 2 月

You know, my philosophy is—it's always been very simple. And it has its flaws, which I'll go into. My philosophy is that everything starts with a great product. So, you know, I obviously believed in listening to customers, but customers can't tell you about the next break through that's going to happen next year that's going to change the whole industry. So you have to listen very carefullY.but then you have to go and sort of stow away—you have to go hide away with people that really understand the technology,but also really care about the customers, and dream up this next breakthrough. And that's my perspective, that everything starts with a great product. And that has its flaws. I have certainly been accused of not listening to the customers enough. And I think there is probably a certain amount of that that's valid.

Newsweek,September 29, 1985

Innovation has nothing to do with how many R&D (Research and Development) dollars you have. When Apple came up with the Mac, IBM was spending at least 100 times more on R&D. It's not about money. It's about the people you have, how you're led, and how much you get it.

Fortune, November 9, 1998

你知道，我的人生观一直很简单，当然也会有些缺点，接下来我会说到。我的人生观就是一切以产品为中心。所以显而易见，我很相信客户的看法，但客户不会告诉你怎样创新，客户不会告诉你明年的产品该怎样才能改变整个业界。所以在你仔细听取客户的意见之后，暗地里还要和那些真正懂得技术的人一起探讨，却也要同时考虑到客户的感受，来进行产品革新。这就是我的观点，一切以优秀的产品为前提。当然，这个想法也有它的缺陷，我就曾被指责过没有足够聆听客户的反响，而我却觉得可能已经听得够多的了。

《新闻周刊》，
1985年9月29日

创新与你拥有多少研发资金无关。当苹果还在研制Mac电脑的时候，IBM已投入了百倍于我们的资金用于研发。这不是钱的问题。它取决于你拥有的人才，你的领导方式以及你有多懂行。

《财富》杂志，
1998年11月9日

We're gambling on our visionand we would rather do that than make"me, too"products. Let some other companies do that. For US, it's always the next dream.

Apple product event for the first Macintosh computer,January24, 1984

When it comes out, Mac is going to be the most incredible computer in the world.

Business Week, 1983

Over 70% of all the computers used in education in this country are Apples. And we feel pretty good about that; we care a lot about the educational processes, which reflects a bit about what our values are as a corporation. And it's also an incredible leverage point for the Apple II.

Steve Jobs speech in Apple's 1984 annual shareholder's meeting

In addition to designing the machine in the last year and a half, we have designed and built the machine to build the machines. We even invested over 20 million dollars to build the computer industry's first automated factory in Fremont California overlooking Ford and GM.

Steve Jobs speech in Apple's 1984 annual shareholder's meeting

It set the technical direction for the entire industry with its mousse, windows, icons, we are seeing imitations, visa on, MS windows, even a rumored IBMwindowing package works.

Steve Jobs speech in Apple's 1984 annual shareholder's meeting

我们总是跟自己赌博，我们宁可这样做，也不愿生产雷同的产品。让其他公司这样做吧。对于我们来说，总会有下一个梦想。

苹果公司MAC电脑发布会，1984年1月24日

Mac问世后，将成为全世界最不可思议的电脑。

《商业周刊》，1983年

在这个国家里，超过70%的用于教育事业的电脑是苹果的。我们为此感到骄傲，我们非常关注教育的过程，这反映了我们作为一个企业的价值观，以及下一代苹果电脑发展的动力来源。

乔布斯在苹果股东大会上的演讲，1984年

在过去的一年半，除了设计这一台机器（麦金塔电脑），我们同时设计并建造了生产机器的设备。我们甚至在加州弗里蒙特投资了超过2000万美元来建造计算机工业界第一个自动化工厂，从工厂可俯瞰福特和通用汽车。

乔布斯在苹果股东大会上的演讲，1984年

Lisa电脑的鼠标、窗口和图标给整个业界指引了技术方向，我们已经看到了模仿者，比如微软的Windows，甚至有人说IBM的视窗包也是。

乔布斯在苹果股东大会上的演讲，1984年

69

No way, there's no way we're slipping! You guys have been working on this stuff for months now. Another couple of weeks isn't going to make that much of a difference. You may as well get it over with. Just make it as good as you can. You better get back to work!

Folklore. org,January 1984

Real artists ship.

Folklore. org,January 1984

When we finally presented it at the shareholders' meeting, everyone in the auditorium gave it a five-minute ovation. What was incredible to me was that I could see the Mac team in the first few rows. It was as though none of us could believe we'd actually finished it. Everyone started crying.

Playboy, February 1, 1985

We think the Mac will sell zillions, but we didn't build the Mac for anybody else. We built it for ourselves. We were the group of people who were going to judge whether it was great or not. We weren't going to go out and do market research. We just wanted to build the best thing we could build.

Playboy, February 1, 1985

My dream is that every person in the world will have their own Apple computer. To do that, we've got to be a great marketing company.

Odyssey: Pepsi to Apple, 1987

不行，我们决不能有任何差错！你们为这事儿已经忙活了好几个月，而接下来几周的工作却没有什么进展，你们本应该赶紧把这件事情处理妥当的，努力做到最好。

Folklore.org，1984年1月

能上市才是真行家。

Folklore.org，1984年1月

当我们最终在股东大会上展示这款产品时，观众席中的每个人给了它长达5分钟的掌声。我能看到坐在前几排的Mac团队，从他们的表情中可以看到，我们都无法相信我们实际上已经完成了这个产品的开发。每个人都激动得泪流满面，不能自已。

《花花公子》杂志，
1985年2月1日

我们预计，苹果Mac电脑的销量将会无穷大。但是，我们并不是为别人来生产Mac电脑的，我们为自己生产。我们就是判定它是好是坏的一群人。我们没有走出去进行市场调查。我们只是想尽我们所能生产最好的产品。

《花花公子》杂志，
1985年2月1日

我的梦想是世界上每个人都能拥有自己的苹果电脑，为了实现这个梦想，我们必须要成为最棒的销售公司。

《冒险历程：从百事到苹果》，
1987年

The most compelling reason for most people to buy a computer for the home will be to link it to a nationwide communications network. We're just in the beginning stages of what will be a truly remarkable breakthrough for most people—as remarkable as the telephone.

Playboy, Februay1, 1985

The point is that people really don't have to understand how computers work. Most people have no concept of how an automatic transmission works, yet they know how to drive a car. You don't have to study physics to understand the laws of motion to drive a car. You don't have to understand any of this stuff to use Macintosh.

Playboy, Februay1, 1985

We just wanted to build the best thing we could build. When you're a carpenter making a beautifulchest of drawers, you're not going to use a piece of plywood on the back, even though it faces the wall and nobody will ever see it. You'll know it's there, So you're going to use a beautiful piece of wood on the back. For you to sleep well at night, the aesthetic, the quality,has to be carried all the way through.

Playboy, Februay1, 1985

对于大多数人来说，最能说服他们为家庭购买电脑的理由将是把电脑连接到一个全国性的通讯网络中。我们现在正处在一项伟大技术的初始阶段，这项技术对大多数人来说将是一个真正巨大的突破，就像电话的出现一样。

《花花公子》杂志，1985年2月1日

人们不需要理解电脑是怎样工作的，多数人对自动换挡器的工作原理都没有概念，但是他们知道如何开车。你学开车，不一定要学习物理来了解运动定律，要使用麦金塔电脑，你不一定要理解这些。

《花花公子》杂志，1985年2月1日

我们只想尽力把东西做到最好。如果你是一个木匠，准备打造一个衣柜，你不会用质量较差的胶合木板来做这个衣柜的背面，尽管它对着墙壁，没有人会看到它。但是，你自己心里清楚。因此，你会用漂亮的木板来做这个衣柜的背面。哪怕只是为了让你自己睡得安心，你也要把质量和美观贯彻始终。

《花花公子》杂志，1985年2月1日

The primary reasons to buy a computer for your home now are that you want to do some business work at home or you want to run educational software for yourself or your children. If you can't justify buying a computer for one of those two reasons, the only other possible reason is that you just want to be computer literate. You know there's something going on, you don't exactly know what it is, so you want to learn. This will change: computers will be essential in the most homes.

Playboy, Februay1, 1985

We attract a different type of person —a person who doesn't want to wait five or ten years to have someone take a giant risk on him or her. Someone who really wants to get in a little over his head and make a little dent in the universe.

Playboy, Februay1, 1985

I was worth over $1,000,000 when I was 23, and over $10,000,000 when I was 24, and over $100,000,000 when I was 25, and it wasn't that important because I never did it for the money.

Rolling Stone, June 16, 1994

You know, my main reaction to this money thing is that it's humorous, all the attention to it, because it's hardly the most insightful or valuable thing that's happened to me in the past ten years. But it makes me feel old, sometimes, when I speak at a campus and I find that what students are most in awe of iS the fact that I'm a millionaire.

Playboy, Februay1, 1985

现在购买家用电脑的主要原因是，你想要在家里处理一些业务，或者你自己或你的孩子要用教育软件。如果你买电脑不是这两个原因中的一个，唯一可能的原因就是，你只是想成为一个电脑通。你知道正在发生一些事情，但不知道究竟是什么，所以你想学习。这种情况会改变：电脑将成为多数家庭的必备品。

《花花公子》杂志，
1985年2月1日

我们吸引了一种与众不同的人 —— 他们不愿意等待五年或十年去让别人在自己身上冒天大的风险。他真心希望可以在宇宙中留下一点印记。

《花花公子》杂志，
1985年2月1日

我23岁时的财富超过100万美元，24岁时超过1000万美元，25岁时超过1亿美元。不过这些数字并不重要，因为我不是为了钱而工作。

《滚石》杂志，
1994年6月16日

你知道，我对金钱这件事儿的反应是觉得很好笑的。我几乎不怎么关注这方面，因为在过去十年中，它对我来说不是最有深度或最有价值的事情。但这也让我觉得自己老了，有时候我去大学里面演讲的时候，我发现学生们对我最敬畏之处是在于我这个百万富翁的身份。

《花花公子》杂志，
1985年2月1日

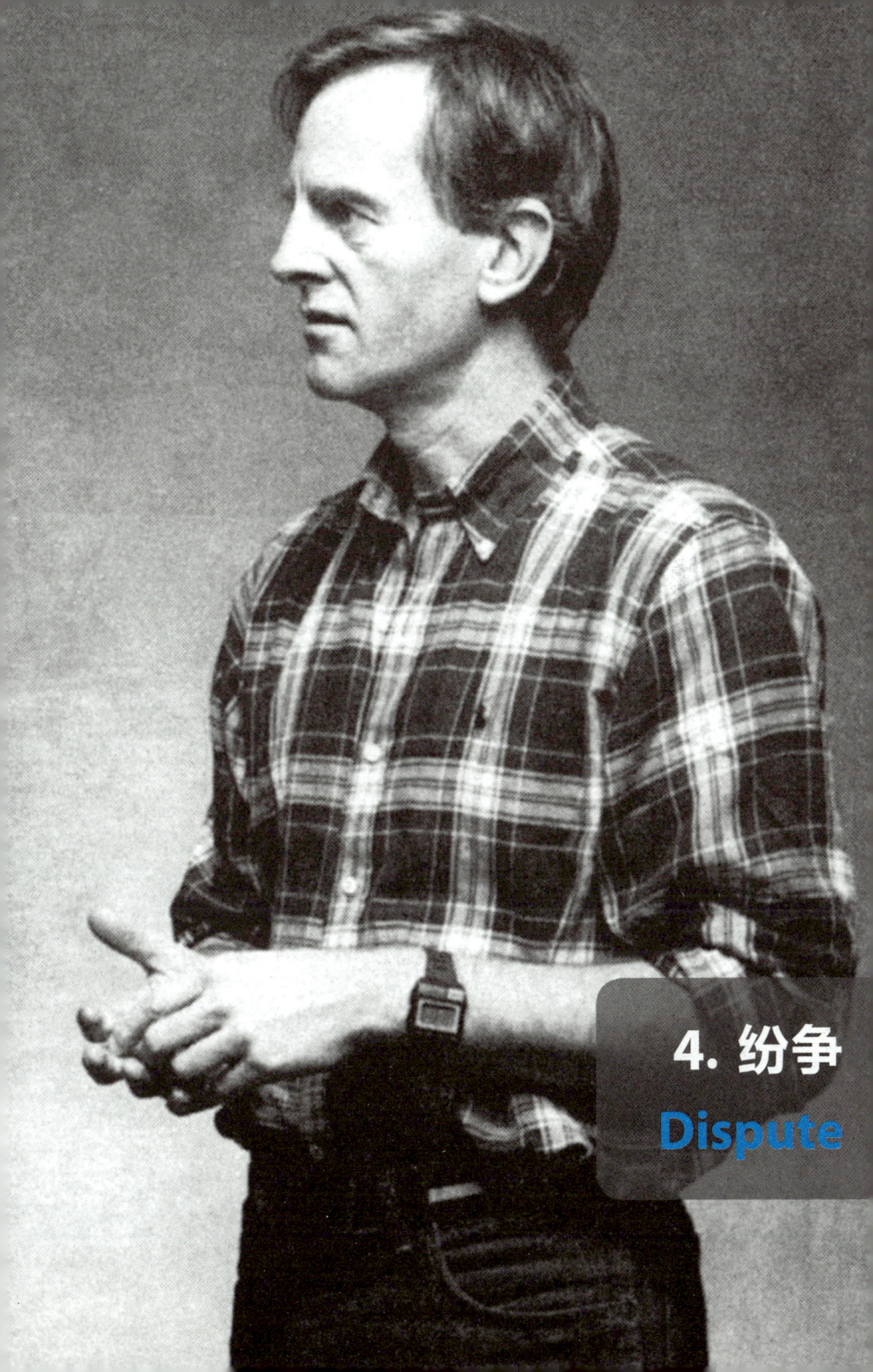

4. 纷争

Dispute

1991年，
乔布斯和比尔·盖茨

In 1991, Steve Jobs and
Bill Gates

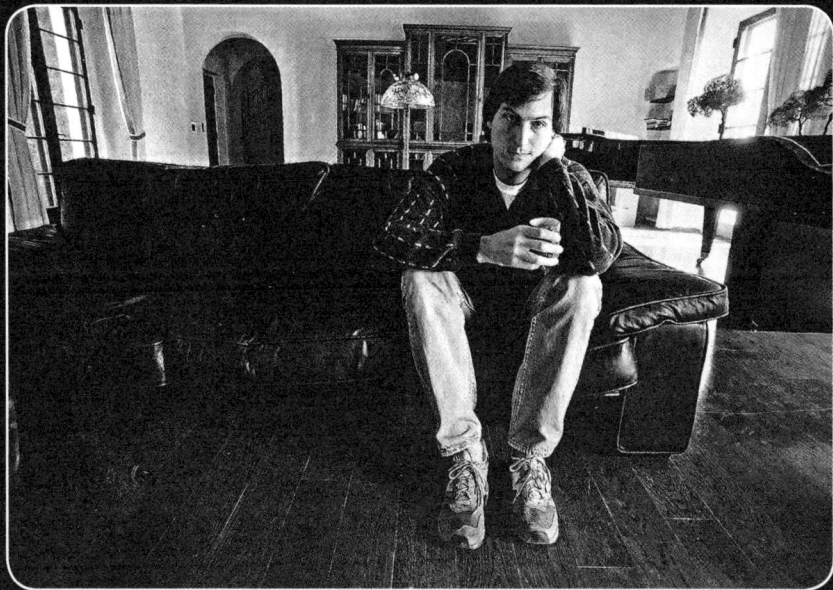

乔布斯在1985年9月21
日拍摄的照片

Steve Jobs poses for a
portrait on September
21, 1985

When I hire somebody really senior, competence is the ante. They have to be really smart. But the real issue for me is, are they going to fall in love with Apple? Because if they fall in love with Apple, everything else will take care of itself.

CNN Money

Do you want to spend the rest of your life selling sugared water or do you want a chance to change the world?

As said to John Sculley

We are inventing the future, Think about surfing on the front edge of a wave. It's really exhilarating. Now think about dog-paddling at the tail end of that wave. It wouldn't be anywhere near as much fun. Come down here and make a dent in the universe.

Steve Jobs,
By Walter Isaacason, 2011

What happens in most companies is that you don't keep great people under working environments where individual accomplishment is discouraged rather than encouraged. The great people leave and you end up with mediocrity, I know,because that's how Apple was built.

Playboy, Februay1, 1985

招聘高层员工时，很难确定他是否能够胜任，这就像赌博。首先，他们必须拥有高智商。但对我来说，问题的关键是，他们是否会热爱苹果公司。如果他们爱苹果公司，就会排除万难，与公司共同进步。

美国有线电视新闻网财经频道

你（约翰·斯卡利）是想用你的余生继续卖糖水呢，还是想得到一个改变世界的机会？

招募前百事总裁
约翰·斯卡利

（说服比尔·阿特金森加入苹果）我们正在创造未来，想象一下在海浪的最前端冲浪是什么感觉，一定很兴奋刺激吧；再想象一下在浪的末尾学狗刨游泳，一点儿意思都没有。来苹果吧，你（比尔·阿特金森）可以吸引全世界的目光。

《史蒂夫·乔布斯传》，
沃尔特·艾萨克森著，
2011 年

对于大多数公司来说，都会发生一个问题，那就是你没办法让优秀人才总是能处于一个适于工作的环境中 —— 一个让他的个人素质得到鼓励而不是打击的环境。于是，优秀人才都走了，最后留下来的都是一些平庸之辈，我之所以会知道，因为苹果就是这样建立起来的。

《花花公子》杂志，
1985 年 2 月 1 日

What ruined Apple was values, John Sculley ruined Apple and he ruined it by bringing a set of values to the top of Apple which were corrupt and corrupted some of the top people who were there, drove out some of the ones who were not corruptible, and brought in more corrupt ones and paid themselves collectively tens of millions of dollars and cared more about their own glory and wealth than they did about what built Apple in the first place—which was making great computers for people to use.

Computerworld Honors Program, 1995

There's an old Hindu saying that goes, "In the first 30 years of your life, you make your habits. For the last 30 years of your life, your habits make you." Come help me celebrate mine.

Invitation of Jobs' birthday party, February 1985

The more the outside world tries to reinforce an image of you, the harder it is to continue to be an artist, which is why a lot of times, artists have to say, "Bye. I have to go. I'm going crazy and I'm getting out of here." And they go and hibernate somewhere. Maybe later they re-emerge a little differently.

Playboy, 1985

I think you really lost your stride, You were really great the first year, and everything went wonderful. But something happened.

Steve Jobs, By Walter Isaacason, 2011

毁掉苹果的是价值观,约翰·斯卡利毁了苹果,他引进了腐败的价值观影响了苹果高层的腐败分子,不肯同流合污的人都被赶走,然后引进更多腐败的家伙。苹果付给这些人数千万美元,但这些人只关心自己的财富和荣耀,而忽视了苹果的基础—— 给人们制造出伟大的电脑用。

《电脑世界荣誉课程》,1995年

有句古老的印度谚语是这样说的,"在人生的头30年里,你养成习惯;在后30年,习惯塑造你。"过来跟我庆祝我的30岁吧。

乔布斯生日派对请柬,1985年2月

外界越是试图强化你的形象,你就越难继续做一名艺术家,这也是为什么很多艺术家要说,"再见,我得走了,我要疯了,我要离开这里。"然后他们就离开了,在某处休隐。也许之后他们又会重新出现,变得有些不同。

《花花公子》,1985年

我觉得你真的已经乱了阵脚,你米苹果的第一年确实很好,一切都很美妙。但是后来出问题了。

《史蒂夫·乔布斯传》,沃尔特·艾萨克森著,2011年

Things don't always happen the way I want them, just like Mick Jagger said, "you can't always get what you want; sometimes you get what you need.

Steve Jobs,
By Walter Isaacason, 2011

the company's recent reorganization left me with no work to do and no access even to regular management reports.

Resignation letter,
September 17, 1985

We worked hard, and in 10 years Apple had grown from just the two of us in a garage into a $2 billion company with over 4000 employees. We had just released our finest creation - the Macintosh - a year earlier, and I had just turned 30. And then I got fired. How can you get fired from a company you started? Well, as Apple grew we hired someone who I thought was very talented to run the company with me, and for the first year or so things went well. But then our visions of the future began to diverge and eventually we had a falling out. When we did, our Board of Directors sided with him. So at 30 I was out. And very publicly out. What had been the focus of my entire adult life was gone, and it was devastating.

Stanford Commencement
Speech, june2005

事情的发展往往不是你想怎么样就能怎么样，就像米克·杰格说的，"你不可能总能得到你想要的东西，有时候你得到你需要的东西就够了"。

《史蒂夫·乔布斯传》，沃尔特·艾萨克森著，2011年

公司近期的重组让我没有工作可做，甚至无法接触到定期的管理报告。

辞职信，1985年9月17日

我们工作得很努力，十年之后，这个公司从那两个车库中的穷光蛋发展到了超过四千名的雇员、价值超过二十亿的大公司。在公司成立的第九年，我们刚刚发布了最好的产品，那就是麦金塔。我也快要到三十岁了。在那一年，我被炒了鱿鱼。你怎么可能被你自己创立的公司炒了鱿鱼呢？嗯，在苹果快速成长的时候，我们雇用了一个很有天分的家伙和我一起管理这个公司，在最初的几年，公司运转的很好。但是后来我们对未来的看法发生了分歧，最终我们吵了起来。当争吵不可开交的时候，董事会站在了他的那一边。所以在三十岁的时候，我被炒了。在这么多人的眼皮下我被炒了。在而立之年，我生命的全部支柱离自己远去，这真是毁灭性的打击。

斯坦福毕业典礼演讲，2005年6月

The board declined to accept my resignation and asked me to defer it for a week. I agreed to do so in light of the encouragement the Board offered with regard to the proposed new venture and the indications that Apple would invest in it. On Friday, after I told John Sculley who would be joining me, he confirmed Apple's willingness to discuss areas of possible collaboration between Apple and my new venture.

Subsequently the company appears to be adopting a hostile posture toward me and the new venture. Accordingly, I must insist upon the immediate acceptance of my resignation. I would hope that in any statement it feels it must issue, the company will make it clear that the decision to resign as chairman was mine.

Resignation letter, September 17, 1985

Screw John Sculley!
Screw the Apple board!
We're going to change the world!

Second Coming of Steve Jobs, 1985

This morning's paper carried suggestions that Apple is considering removing me as chairman... I am but 30 and want still to contribute and achieve. After what we have accomplished together, I would wish our parting to be both amicable and dignified.

Resignation letter, September 17, 1985

董事会拒绝接受我的辞呈，并叫我推迟一个星期再提出。由于公司董事会对我成立新公司的计划给予了一定的鼓励，苹果公司也打算对我的新公司进行投资，因此我就同意了推迟提出辞职。星期五，在我告诉约翰·斯卡利谁将加入我的新公司后，他声称苹果公司愿意讨论、协商与我新创建的公司之间在某些领域可以开展的合作。

但随后，公司好像又对我和我的新公司采取了敌视的态度。相应地，我必须坚持我的辞呈马上被批准。我希望苹果公司的任何生命都是被迫发表的，我也希望苹果公司能明白是我首先提出辞去董事会主席这一职务的。

辞职信，1985年9月17日

让约翰·斯卡利见鬼去吧！
让苹果董事会见鬼去吧！
我们要改变世界！

《追随内心》，1985年

我从今天早晨的报纸上得知，苹果公司正在考虑把我从董事会主席的位置上赶下去……我只有30岁，我还想为电脑事业贡献自己的力量，也希望取得一定的成就。我们毕竟在一起取得了那么大的成就，我衷心希望我们的分离是友善的，也是让人愉快的。

辞职信，1985年9月17日

If Apple becomes a place where computers are a commodity item, where the romance is gone, and where people forget that computers are the most incredible invention that man has ever invented, I'LL feel I have lost Apple. But if I'm a million miles away,and all those people still feel those things... then I will feel that my genes are still there.

Newsweek,
September 29,1985

I really didn't know what to do for a few months. I felt that I had let the previous generation of entrepreneurs down - that I had dropped the baton as it was being passed to me. I met with David Packard and Bob Noyce and tried to apologize for screwing up so badly. I was a very public failure, and I even thought about running away from the valley. But something slowly began to dawn on me – I still loved what I did. The turn of events at Apple had not changed that one bit. I had been rejected, but I was still in love. And so I decided to start over.

Stanford Commencement Speech, June2005

如果苹果公司变成了一个把电脑只当成商品的地方，所有的浪漫情怀就会消失殆尽，人们也会忘记了电脑是人类最不可思议的发明，如果是这样的话，我会感到我已经失去了苹果。但如果我离开之后，所有的苹果人还能感到浪漫的情怀，感到电脑是最不可思议的发明……我会觉得我的精神仍在这里，从未离开。

《新闻周刊》，
1985 年 9 月 29 日

　　在最初的几个月里，我真是不知道该做些什么。我把从前的创业激情给丢了，我觉得自己让与我一同创业的人都很沮丧。我和 David Pack 和 Bob Noyce 见面，并试图向他们道歉。我把事情弄得糟糕透顶了。但是我渐渐发现了曙光，我仍然喜爱我从事的这些东西。苹果公司发生的这些事情丝毫的没有改变这些，一点也没有。我被驱逐了，但是我仍然钟爱它。所以我决定从头再来。

斯坦福毕业典礼演讲，
2005 年 6 月

I wasn't aware that Apple owned me, you know. I don't think they do. I think that I own me. And for me not to be able to practice my craft ever again in my life seems odd. We're not going to take any technology, any proprietary ideas out of Apple. We're willing to put that in writing. It's the law, anyway. There is nothing, by the way, that says Apple can't compete with US if they think what we're doing is such a great idea. It's hard to think that a $2 billion company with 4, 300+people couldn't compete with six people in blue jeans.

Newsweek,
September 30,1985

I didn't see it then, but it turned out that getting fired from Apple was the best thing that could have ever happened to me. The heaviness of being successful was replaced by the lightness of being a beginner again, less sure about everything. It freed me to enter one of the most creative periods of my life.

Stanford Commencement Speech, June2005

What I'm best at doing is finding a group of talented people and making things with them. I respect the direction that Apple is going in. but for me personally, you know, I want to make things, and if there's no place for me to make things there, then I'll do what I did twice before, I'll make my own place.

Newsweek, 1985

（苹果管理层对我带领留六名员工去研发 NeXT 一事颇有怨言，对此，我说道：）我不认为我是属于苹果的，我也不认为他们（六名员工）是属于苹果的，我就是我自己的。对我来说，手艺无处施展才是邪门的事儿。苹果公司不会把任何技术、任何一个专有想法拒之门外。我希望可以把这句话写下来，这是原则。如果他们觉得我们正在实现的是一个伟大的创意，苹果公司当然可以和我们来竞争。很难想象，堂堂一个拥有 20 亿美金资产和超过 4300 名员工的大公司会斗不过六个穿着牛仔裤的人。

《新闻周刊》杂志，1985 年 12 月 30 日

我当时没有觉察，但是事后证明，从苹果公司被炒是我这辈子发生的最棒的事情。因为，作为一个成功者的极乐感觉被作为一个创业者的轻松感觉所重新代替：对任何事情都不那么特别看重。这让我觉得如此自由，进入了我生命中最有创造力的一个阶段。

斯坦福毕业典礼演讲，2005 年 6 月

我最擅长的事情就是召集一群天才般的人，和他们一起设计产品。我尊重苹果公司所做的发展选择，但对于我个人来说，我还是想设计出更多的产品。如果苹果公司容不下我设计自己的东西，我就会和以前一样自己单干。我会开拓属于自己的地盘。

《新闻周刊》，1985 年

I had ten of the best years of my life, you know, and I don't regret much of anything. I want to get on with my life.

Newsweek, 1985

I'll always stay connected with Apple. I hope that throughout my life I'll sort of have the thread of my life and the thread of Apple weave in and out of each other, like a tapestry. There may be a few years when I'm not there, but I'll always come back.

*Playboy, Februay*1, 1985

IBM wants to wipe US offthe face of the earth.

Fortune, February 20,1984

Welcome, IBM. Seriously…And congratulations on your first personal computer. Putting real computing power in the hands of the individual is already improving the way people work, think, learn, communicate, and spend their leisure hours. Computer literacy is fast becoming as fundamental a skill as reading or writing.

Apple print ad in the Wall Street Journal, August24, 1981

It's curious to me that the largest computer company in the world [IBM] couldn't even match the Apple II, which was designed in a garage six years ago.

InfoWorld, March8 1982

在苹果公司，我度过了我一生中最值得留恋的10年光阴，我对我所做的任何事情从来没有后悔过。在以后的岁月里，我还是要继续我的生活。

《新闻周刊》，1985年

我会始终与苹果保持联系。我希望在我的整个人生中，我能将我人生的丝线与苹果的丝线交织在一起，就像地毯一样。有几年时间我不在苹果，但是我最终将会回来。

《花花公子》杂志，1985年2月1日

我们的竞争对手IBM想把我们从地球上清除出去。

《财富》杂志，1984年2月20日

真诚地欢迎你，IBM—— 祝贺你制造出了你们的第一台个人电脑。个人拥有了真正的计算机能力，这改变了人们的工作、思考、学习、交流以及休闲娱乐的方式。使用计算机的能力很快就变成了了阅读、写作一样的基本技能。

苹果刊登在《华尔街日报》上的广告，1981年8月24日

有个问题一直让我觉得很奇怪，世界上最大的电脑公司（IBM）竟然打不过Apple Ⅱ—— 一个六年前在车库中创办的公司。

《信息世界》杂志，1982年3月8日

The shakeout is in full swing. The first major firm goes bankrupt, with others teetering on the brink. Total industry losses for 1983 overshadow even the combined profits of Apple and IBM for personal computers. It is now 1984. It appears IBM wants it all. Apple is perceived to be the only hope to offer IBM a run for its money. Dealers initially welcoming IBM with open arms now fear an IBM dominated and controlled future. They've increasingly and desperately turning back to Apple as the only force that can insure their future freedom.

Steve Jobs speech on IBM in 1983

I am saddened, not by Microsoft's success — I have no problem with their success. They've earned their success, for the most part. I have a problem with the fact that they just make really third-rate products.

Triumph of the Nerds, 1996

The desktop computer industry is dead. Innovation has virtually ceased. Microsoft dominates with very little innovation. That's over. Apple lost. The desktop market has entered the dark ages, and it's going to be in the dark ages for the next 10 years, or certainly for the rest of this decade.

Wired, February 1996

当时正值行业调整的风头上。第一家大公司破产后，很多其他公司也处于破产的边缘。1983年整个行业的亏损额等于苹果及IBM个人电脑的总利润。现在是1984年。IBM想把一切据为己有。苹果被认为是为IBM提供运营资金的唯一希望。最初对IBM表示热烈欢迎的供应商现在害怕由IBM主导和控制未来。越来越多的公司在绝望中求助于苹果，认为它是唯一能保证它们未来自由的力量。

史蒂夫·乔布斯针对IBM的演讲，1983年

我感到很沮丧，但不是因为微软的成功——我一点儿也不担心他们的成功。我感到沮丧的原因是，尽管微软总体上来说取得了成功，但是他们只做出了三流的产品。

《书呆子的胜利》，1996年

台式电脑行业已经完了。创新几乎停滞了。微软占据了首要的位置，却只有极少量的创新。那就完了。苹果迷失了。台式机市场进入了黑暗时代，这将延续10年，或者至少延续到这个十年末。

《连线》杂志，1996年2月

Eventually, Microsoft will crumble because of complacency, and maybe some new things will grow. But until that happens, until there's some fundamental technology shift, it's just over.

Wired, February 1996

The only problem with Microsoft is they just have no taste. They have absolutely no taste. And I don't mean that in a small way, I mean that in a big way, in the sense that they don't think of original ideas, and they don't bring much culture into their products.

Triumph of the Nerds, 1996

最终，微软将会因为骄傲自满而土崩瓦解。到那个时候，也许会有一些新的事物得到发展。但是，等到那个时候，等到出现一些基本的技术革新，整个行业已经结束了。

《连线》杂志，1996年2月

微软的唯一问题就是他们没有什么品位。他们是真的没有品位。我不是从小的方面来说的，而是从大的方面来说的。我是说他们从来不去想产品设计的本意，也没有带给产品多少文化内涵。

《书呆子的胜利》，1996年

5. 重建
Rebuild

乔布斯和NeXT创办者
的合影，1986年

Steve Jobs with
founders of NeXT, 1986

1997年史蒂夫·乔布斯
和妻子劳伦·鲍威尔在
自家后院

Steve Jobs and his wife
Laurene Powell, taken in
their own backyard,1997

It's rare that you see an artist in his 30s or 40s able to really contribute something amazing. Of course, there are some people who are innately curious, forever little kids in their awe of life, but they're rare.

Playboy, 1985

I'm the only person I know that's lost a quarter of a billion dollars in one year...It's very character-building.

Apple Confidential 2.0

During the next five years, I started a company named NeXT, another company named Pixar, and fell in love with an amazing woman who would become my wife.

Stanford Commencement Speech, June2005

I was in the parking lot, with the key in the car,and I thought to myself: If this is my last night on earth, would I rather spend it at a business meeting or with this woman?I ran across the parking lot, asked her if she'd have dinner with me. She said yes, we walked into town, and we've been together eversince.

New York Times Magazine, January 12, 1997

In most people's vocabularies, design means veneer. It's interior decorating. It's the fabric of the curtains of the sofa. But to me, nothing could be further from the meaning of design. Design is the fundamental soul of a human-made creation that ends up expressing itself in successive outer layers of the product or service.

Playboy,1987

你很少能见到有艺术家在三、四十岁时还能够创造一些真正令人惊讶的作品。当然，有人天生就有好奇心，一辈子都像小孩一样，但这种人很少。

《花花公子》杂志，1985年

我是我所知道的唯一一个在一年中失去2.5亿美元的人……这对我的成长很有帮助。

《苹果揭秘》

在接下来的五年里，我创立了一个名叫NeXT的公司，还有一个叫Pixar的公司，然后和一个后来成为我妻子的优雅女人相识。

斯坦福毕业典礼演讲，2005年6月

（谈到和妻子劳伦的相遇）我把车钥匙锁在了车里，在停车场待了很久，我对自己说，如果这是我活在人世的最后一晚，我应该如何度过？——开会？还是和这个女人一起度过？于是我跑出停车场，问她说是不是愿意和我一起吃个饭，她说好啊，之后我们一起走路去了城里，相伴直到现在。

《纽约时报》杂志，1997年1月12日

在大多数人的字典中，设计意味着华丽的虚饰，是室内装潢，是沙发皮质的面料。但对我来说，没有什么能远离设计。设计是产品的灵魂，灵魂通过产品和服务的外观表达自己。

《花花公子》杂志，1987年

It's not about pop culture, and it's not about fooling people, and it's not about convincing people that they want something they don't. We figure out what we want. And I think we're pretty good at having the right discipline to think through whether a lot of other people are going to want it, too. That's what we get paid to do.

CNN Money

Look at the Mercedes design, the proportion of sharp detail to flowing lines. Over the years they've made the design softer but the details starker. That's what we have to do with the Macintosh.

Odyssey: Pepsi to Apple, 1987

If I knew in 1986 how much it was going to cost to keep Pixar going, I doubt if I would have bought the company.

Fortune

Apple has some pretty amazing people, but the collection of people at Pixar is the highest concentration of remarkable people I have ever witnessed.There's a person who's got a Ph. D. in computer—generated plants—3D grass and trees and flowers. There's another who iS the best in the world at putting imagery on film. Also, Pixar is more multidisciplinary than Apple ever will be. But the key thing is that it is much smaller. Pixar's got 450 people. You could never have the collection of people that Pixar has now if you went to two thousand people.

CNNMoney / Fortune, November 9, 1998

不是源于流行文化，不是欺骗大众，不是劝说人们购买他们不需要的产品。我们要设计自己想要的产品。同时，我认为我们擅长判断多数人是否也需要这种产品。这是我们应该做的。

美国有线电视新闻网财经频道

看看梅赛德斯的设计吧，流线型线条中那些锐利的细节。许多年过去了，他们的设计变得更加柔和，但细节也变得更加朴实无华。我们设计的Mac机也应该如此。

《冒险历程：从百事到苹果》，1987 年

如果我在 1986 年知道经营皮克斯公司需要花费多少资金的话，我就得考虑到底应该不应该购买这家公司。

《财富》杂志

苹果公司的员工的确都很出色，但皮克斯的员工更是"好中之好"。那里有专门研究电脑特技的博士，可以做出来 3D 效果的花草树木，还有世界上技术最好的在电影中放入图像的工程师。不仅如此，和苹果比起来，皮克斯的涉猎范围更大，但关键性的东西更少。皮克斯有 450 名员工，但如果你去了有 2000 个员工的公司，也找不到这么出色的团队。

美国有线电视新闻网财经频道/《财富》杂志，1998 年 9 月 9 日

Pixar's got by far and away the best computer graphics talent in the entire world, and it now has the best animation and artistic talent in the whole world to do these kinds of film. There's really no one else in the world who could do this stuff. It's really phenomenal. We're probably close to ten years ahead of anybody else.

Smithsonian Institution Oral and Video Histories, April 20,1995

What a computer is to me is the most remarkable tool that we have ever come up with. It's the equivalent of a bicycle for our minds.

Memory&Imagination, 1990

Being the richest man in the cemetery doesn't matter to me … Going to bed at night saying we've done something wonderful… that's what matters to me.

The *Wall Street Journal*, May 25, 1993

There's no yacht in my future, I've never done this for the money.

New York Times, 1995

One of the reasons I think Microsoft took ten years to copy the Mac is 'cause they didn't really get it at its core.

Rolling Stone, June16,1994

Innovation has virtually ceased, Microsoft dominates with very little innovation. Apple lost. The desktop market has entered the dark ages.

Wired, 1995

纵观整个世界，皮克斯公司是最优秀的电脑绘图公司，它拥有世界上最出色的艺术人才和动画片绘制人才。它拍摄的电影是其他公司望尘莫及的。皮克斯确实是个非凡的公司，我们领先于其他同行大概十年的时间。

史密森学会，口述和视频记录，1995年4月20日

电脑对我而言，是一种最非凡的工具，在我心中，它和自行车的地位是一样的。

《记忆与想象》，1990年

成为坟墓中最有钱的人，对我来说毫无意义；晚上上床睡觉前能够说声我们已漂亮地干完了活儿，这对于我来说妙不可言。

《华尔街日报》，1993年5月25日

我的未来不需要游艇，我做这个从来都不是为了钱。

纽约时报，1995年

我觉得微软花了十年时间抄袭苹果，原因之一，就是因为他们不曾真正抄到苹果的核心技术。

《滚石》杂志，1994年6月16日

创新实际上已经停止了，微软占据了市场，但几乎没有创新。苹果输了，台式电脑市场进入了黑暗时代。

《连线》杂志，1995年

In Our business, one person can't do anything anymore. You create a team of people around you. You have a responsibility of integrity of work to that team. Everybody does try to turn out the best work that they can.

Smithsonian Institution Oral and Video Histories, April 20,1995

It's painful when you have some people who are not the best people in the world and you have to get rid of them; but I found my job has sometimes exactly been that—to get rid of some people who didn't measure up and I've always tried to do it in a humane way. But nonetheless it has to be done and it is never fun.

Smithsonian Institution Oral and Video Histories, April 20, 1995

I think the artistry is in having an insight into what one sees around them. Generally putting things together in a way no one else has before and finding a way to express that to other people who don't have that insight…

Smithsonian Institution Oral and Video Histories, April20,1995

Creativity is just connecting things. When you ask creative people how they did something, they feel a little guilty because they didn't really do it, they just saw something. It seemed obvious to them after a while. That's because they were able to connect experiences they've had and synthesize new things. And the reason they were able to do that was that they've had more experiences or they have thought more about their experiences than other people.

Wired, February 1996

在我们这个行业，一个人不可能单枪匹马完成所有事情。你需要组建一支团队来帮助你，你有为这个团队忠诚工作的责任，每个人都会努力做到最好。

史密森学会，口述和视频记录，1995年4月20日

如果你的员工不是世界上最优秀的，这是个让人伤脑筋的事情，因为你不得不去把他们处理掉。而我有时候面对的正是这样的工作—— 开除那些不合格的员工，我做的尽可能人性化一点，但无论如何，这是必须要做的事情，而且毫无乐趣可言。

史密森学会，口述和视频记录，1995年4月20日

在我看来，艺术就是有洞察身边一切事物的好眼光。用前人没有用过的方式，把东西组合在一起，再把它呈现给那些没有这个好眼光的人看。

史密森学会，口述和视频记录，1995年4月20日

创新就是把各种事物整合到一起。当你问有创意的人是如何创新的，他们可能会感到一丝负罪感，因为他们根本就没有创造什么，他们只是看到了一些联系。他们总能一眼就看出各种事物之间的联系，因为他们习惯于将他们的各种经验联系起来，然后整合形成新的东西。他们之所以能够做到这一点，是因为他们具有比别人更加丰富的经验，或者他们对自己的经验思考得更多。

《连线》杂志，1996年2月

Design is a funny word. Some people think design means how it looks. But of course, if you dig deeper, it's really how it works. The design of the Mac wasn't what it looked like, although that was part of it. Primarily, it was how it worked.

Wired, February 1996

To design something really well, you have to get it. You have to really grok what it's all about. It takes a passionate commitment to really thoroughly understand something, chew it up, not just quickly swallow it. Most people don't take the time to do that.

Wired, February 1996

Unfortunately, that's too rare a commodity. A lot of people in our industry haven't had very diverse experiences. So they don't have enough dots to connect, and they end up with very linear solutions without a broad perspective on the problem. The broader one's understanding of the human experience, the better design we will have.

Wired, February 1996

设计是一个有趣的词。有人认为，设计就是设计对象的外观。但是细究起来，它还包括设计对象的工作方式。苹果Mac电脑的设计就不仅仅包括它的外观，尽管外观也是设计的一部分。它的设计主要还是它的工作方式。

《连线》杂志，1996年2月

要把某个东西设计得很好，你就必须熟悉它，真正了解它到底是什么。你需要持续投入很大的热情才能真正彻底地明白它，你需要反复地咀嚼回味，而不只是囫囵吞枣。但是，大多数人不愿意花时间这样做。

《连线》杂志，1996年2月

不幸的是，这是一种非常稀缺的品质。我们行业中的很多人缺乏多方面的经验。因此，他们就没有很多点可供联系，对待问题就只能提出线性的解决方案，而没有宽广的视野。我们对于人类的体验了解得更深更广，我们的设计就会越出色。

《连线》杂志，1996年2月

Ultimately, it comes down to taste. It comes down to trying to expose yourself to the best things that humans have done and then try to bring those things in to what you're doing. Picasso had a saying: good artists copy, great artists steal. And we have always been shameless about stealing great ideas, and I think part of what made the Macintosh great was that the people working on it were musicians and poets and artists and zoologists and historians who also happened to be the best computer scientists in the world.

Triumph of the Nerds, PBS, June 1996

The desktop metaphor was invented because one, you were a stand-alone device, and two, you had to manage your own storage. That's a very big thing in a desktop world. And that may go away. You may not have to manage your own storage. You may not store much before too long.

Wired, February 1996

I'm an optimist in the sense that I believe humans are noble and honorable, and some of them are really smart. I have a very optimistic view of individuals. As individuals, people are inherently good. I have a somewhat more pessimistic view of people in groups. And I remain extremely concerned when I see what's happening in our country. We don't seem to be excited about making our country a better place for our kids.

Wired, February 1996

最后，其实归根到底是品位的问题。你要尽量让自己接触到这个世界上最优秀的产品，并把它运用到自己的工作中去。毕加索说过："好的艺术家复制，伟大的艺术家偷窃。"当我们剽窃别人的卓越的创意的时候，从不觉得着愧，而且我觉得Mac之所以能成为一件卓越的产品，原因之一就是创造它的人中有音乐家、诗人、动物学家、历史学家——而他们碰巧成了世界上最出色的电脑科学家。

美国国家广播公司《小人物的胜利》，1996年7月

　　台式电脑的寓意是：其一，你的设备是独立的；其二，你需要自己管理你存储的东西。这是台式电脑世界中最为关键的理念。这一切可能会一去不复返了。你不必要管理你自己存储的东西。在不久的将来，你可能不必存储很多东西。

《连线》杂志，1996年2月

　　在某种意义上，我是一个乐观主义者。我相信人类是高贵的，值得尊敬的，其中还有一些人绝顶聪明。我对个人充满了乐观的态度。作为个体，人本质上是好的。但是，我对于群体中的人持有一种悲观的态度。当我看到我们国家发生的一些事情时，我感到非常担心。我们似乎怎么也无法让我们的国家变成一个更适合我们孩子生活的地方。

《连线》杂志，1996年2月

We have always been shameless about stealing great ideas.

PBS Documentary, Triumph of the Nerds, 1996

I wish him (Bill Gates) the best, I really do. I just think he and Microsoft are a bit narrow. He'd be a broader guy if he had dropped acid once or gone off to an ashram when he was younger."

The New York Times, January12, 1997

These technologies can make life easier, can let us touch people we might not otherwise. You may have a child with a birth defect and be able to get in touch with other parents and support groups, get medical information, the latest experimental drugs. These things can profoundly influence life. I'm not downplaying that.

Wired, February 1996

About 25% of it is totally me, right down to the mannerisms, And I'm certainly not telling you which 25%.

New York Times, 1996

我们窃取他人的奇思妙想，并且从不羞愧。

1996 年的美国公共电视网播出的电视纪录片《书呆子的胜利》

我衷心祝愿他（比尔·盖茨），真的。我只是觉得微软和盖茨狭隘。如果能放下尖酸刻薄或者年轻的时候修身养性，那么他的心胸一定会变得更加开阔。

《纽约时报》，1997 年 1 月 12 日

技术能让生活变得更轻松，能让我们联系到我们以前联系不到的人。例如，假设你有一个孩子具有先天性缺陷，你就能通过这些技术与其他的父母和医疗团队取得联系，获得最新的医学资讯和最新研制的药品。在这些方面，技术能够深刻地影响我们的生活。我一点也没有小瞧它们。

《连线》杂志，1996 年 2 月

这个角色的 25% 左右完全是我，直指我那些怪癖，当然我不会告诉你是哪 25%。

《纽约时报》，1996 年

6. 回归
Return

在波士顿的Macworld大
会演讲前几小时，乔布
斯和盖茨在电话中敲定
了与微软的合作

In a few hours before the
Macworld Conference
in Boston to deliver a
speech, Jobs and Gates
finalize a partnership
with Microsoft on the
phone

1997年，苹果公司在乔布斯的治理下重塑了团队氛围

In 1997, Jobs governance remodeled team atmosphere in Apple

What if Apple didn't exist?Think about it. Time wouldn't get published next week.Some 70% of the newspapers in the U. S. wouldn't publish tomorrow morning. Some 60% of the kids wouldn't have computers; 64% of the teachers wouldn't have computers. More than half the Websites created on Macs wouldn't exist. So there's something worth saving here. See?

Time, August 18,1997

Apple bought NeXT and I returned to Apple and the technology we developed at NeXT is at the heart of Apple's current renaissance.

Stanford Commencement Speech, June2005

This Apple thing is that way for me. I don't want to fail, of course. But even though I didn't't'know how bad things really were, I still had a lot to think about before I said yes. I had to consider the implications for Pixar, for my family, for my reputation. I decided that I didn't really care. because this is what I want to do. If I try my best and fail, well, I've tried my best.

CNNMoney / Fortune, November 9, 1998

如果苹果消失，世界将会怎样？好好想想吧。《时代》杂志下周将不会出版，美国70%的报纸第二天都将停发，60%的孩子和64%的老师将不会拥有个人电脑。一半以上用mac创建的网站也将不复存在。看到了吧，苹果的存在，事关重大。

《时代》杂志，
1997年8月18日

　　苹果电脑买下了NeXT，我回到了苹果公司，我们在NeXT研发的技术成了苹果电脑后来复兴的核心。

斯坦福毕业典礼演讲，
2005年6月

　　苹果对我来说就是这样。我当然不希望失败，但即便我不知道未来会有什么坏事发生，在说"好的"之前，我仍然会前思后想很久。我必须考虑这件事对皮克斯有什么影响，对我的家庭有什么影响，对我自己的声誉有什么影响，但最后我还是会做，我决定不能这么畏首畏尾，因为这是我真正想做的事情。如果我尽力之后还是失败了，无所谓，因为我努力过了。

美国有线电视新闻网财经
频道/《财富》杂志，
1998年9月9日

What are the great brands? Levi's, Coke, Disney, Nike. Most people would put Apple in that category. You could spend billions of dollars building a brand not as good as Apple. Yet Apple hasn't been doing anything with this incredible asset. What is Apple, after all? Apple is about people who think"outside the box, "people who want to use computers to help them change the world, to help them create things that make a difference, and not just to get a job done.

Time, August 18,1997

Apple has some tremendous assets, but I believe without some attention, the company could, could. could—I'm searching for the right word—could, could die.

Time, August 18,1997

Apple was about 90 days away from going bankrupt back then, in the early days and, ti was much worse than I thought when I went back, initially. But there were people there who I'd expected all the good people would have left, and I found these miraculous people, these great people and I said "why?" t tired to ask this as tactfully as I could but "why are you still here?" And, you know, a lot of them had this little phrase they said "I, because I believed in six colors, which was the old six color Apple logo, and, that was code for "because I love what this place stands for" or at least stood for.

interview at D8 in 2010

什么是名牌？里维斯、可口可乐、迪士尼、耐克都是。很多人也会把苹果归入此列。也许你花重金想打造一个品牌，到头来却远不及苹果有名，但是苹果品牌的建立从未花过很多钱。说到底，苹果是什么？ 苹果是那些"跳到盒子外面"去思考问题的人们提供的品牌，那些希望通过电脑来帮助自己改变世界的人们提供的品牌，是那些想要进行创造活动，有所作为，而不仅仅机械工作的人提供的品牌。

《时代》杂志，
1997年8月18日

苹果确实拥有庞大的资产，但我相信，如果不能引起关注，这个公司很可能，可能，可能 —— 让我找个合适的词 —— 可能会死去。

《时代》杂志，
1997年8月18

那时候苹果只能坚持三个月左右就会破产了，我刚回去时，情况比我想象的更糟糕，但是仍有些人坚守岗位。我本以为这些优秀的人会离开的，但是我找到了这些令人惊奇的人、这些伟大的人．我问"为什么"我尽量巧妙地问"为什么你们会留下来？"很多人的回答非常简短，他们说"因为我相信六色"—— 就是苹果老代的六色商标，这等于说"我喜欢这个地方所代表的东西"，至少是曾经代表的东西。

D8峰会上的访谈，2010年

When I started to get involved, a lot of people gave me advice, and some of the most popular advice was, "Apple has become irrelevant." There was a great one that was, "Apple can't execute anything." And another one was, "the Apple culture is anarchy. No one could manage it." You've read all these things in the press. After four weeks, here is what I found quite the opposite of these things, actually. Apple's not as relevant as it used to be everywhere, but in some incredibly important market segments it's extraordinarily relevant.

Steve Jobs' speech for his return in 1997

Many times in an interview I will purposely upset someone: I'll criticize   their prior work. I'll do my homework, find out what they worked on, and say, "God, that really turned out to be a bomb. That really turned out to be a bozo product. Why did you work on that?…"I want to see what people are like under pressure. I want to see if they just fold or if they have firm conviction, belief,and pride in what they did.

In the Company of Giants, 1997

When I got back here in l997 I was looking for more room, and I found an archive of old Macs and other stuff. I shipped all that off to Stanford. If you look backward in this business, you'll be crushed. You have to look forward.

Wired, December 22, 2008

当我刚准备回到苹果的时候，很多人给了我建议。其中最普遍的说法就是"苹果已经过时了"；还有甚者，认为"苹果完全没有执行力"；另外还提到说"苹果的企业文化很混乱，已无可救药"——这些说法你们肯定都在新闻里读到过。然而四个星期之后，我发现，事实完全相反。虽然苹果可能已没有先前那般无处不在的影响力，但在一些核心的市场领域，它仍然占据着举足轻重的地位。

乔布斯回归苹果的演讲，1997 年

很多时候，我在采访的时候，常常会故意表现得惹人讨厌：我会批评他们的前期准备工作，我会自己做做功课，看看他们之前干了什么，还会说："天哪，那个真是太失败了，真是个笨蛋产品啊，你为什么要做这个呢？……"我想看到的是人们在压力下会有什么样的表现，是一击即垮，还是对自己所做的有坚定信念并感到自豪。

《巨人公司》，1997 年

1997 年，我重回苹果公司之后，开始寻找更多的机会。我找到了很多老 Mac 机和其他一堆东西的档案，我把这些东西统统送去了斯坦福。如果你总是频频回顾，你会被击垮的，你必须向前看。

《连线》杂志，2008 年 12 月 22 日

Apple lives in an ecosystem, and it needs help from other partners. It needs to help other partners. Relationships that are destructive don't help anybody in this industry as it is today. So during the last several weeks we have looked at some of the relationships. One has stood out as a relationship that hasn't been going so well, but has the potential, I think, to be great for both companies. I'd like to announce one or our first partnerships today, a very very meaningful one, and that is one with Microsoft.

Steve Jobs' speech for his return in 1997

You know where we're right now is we're shepherding some of the greatest assets in the computer industry. And if we want to move forward and see Apple healthy and prospering again, we have to let go of a few things here. We have to let go of this notion that for Apple to win Microsoft has to lose. We have to embrace embrace the notion that for Apple to win, Apple has to do a really good job. And if others are going to help us, that's great. Because we need all the help we can get. And if we screw up or we don't do a good job, it's not somebody else's fault. It's our fault. So I think that's a very important perspective.

Steve Jobs' speech for his return in 1997

Nobody has tried to swallow us since I've been here. I think they are afraid how we would taste.

Apple shareholder meeting, April 22, 1998

苹果生存在一个生态系统中，它需要来自其他合作伙伴的帮助，也需要去帮助其他合作伙伴。如今，关系的毁坏对这个行业中的任何人都没有好处。所以在前几周里，我们找到了一些合作关系，其中一个存在潜力但之前并没有被开发的合作关系突显了出来，我认为这对我们两个公司均有益处。而我想在今天向你们介绍我们的首位的合作伙伴，非常非常有意义的一个合作伙伴。这个合作伙伴就是微软。

乔布斯回归苹果的演讲，1997年

你们知道，你我现在做的，是我们对计算机行业最伟大资产的引导。如果我们想要继续前进，看到苹果公司重获健康与繁荣，我们就必须在这里放下一些事情，我们必须放弃苹果要赢而微软就得输的这种观念。我们必须怀揣着让苹果重新获胜这一信念，苹果必须去做到极致。并且如果其他人也愿意帮助我们，那就太棒了，因为我们需要一切我们能获得的帮助。但如果是我们自己搞砸了，自己的工作没有做好，那么那不是任何人的错。而是我们自己的错。所以我们想这是一个非常重要的认识。

乔布斯回归苹果的演讲，1997年

自从我回来，就没有公司敢吞掉我们，他们害怕我们的味道。

苹果公司股东会议，1998年4月22日

If we could make four great product platforms that's all we need. We can put our A team on every single one of them instead of having a B or a C team on any. We can turn them much faster.

Keynote address, Seybold Seminars, March 1998

I think the people that do buy them do think differently. They are the creative spirits in this world. They are the people that are not just out to get a job, but they're out to change the world. They're out to change the world using whatever great tools they can get. And we make tools for those kinds of people.

Steve Jobs' speech for his return in 1997

It's not just recruiting. After recruiting, it's building an environment that makes people feel they are surrounded by equally talented people and their work is bigger than they are. The feeling that the work will have tremendous influence and iS part of a strong, clear vision—all those things. Recruiting usually requires more than you alone can do, So I've found that collaborative recruiting and having a culture that recruits the"A"players is the best way. Any interviewee will speak with at least a dozen people in several areas of this company not just those in the area that he would work in. That way a lot of your'A'employees get broad exposure to the company and—by having a company culture that supports them if they feel strongly enough—the current employees can veto a candidate.

In the Company of Giants, 1997

我们最大的希望，是能够开发出来四个出色的产品平台。我们可以把精英部队全部安排到这些项目中去，这样开发速度可以快得多。

Seybold研讨会上的发言，1998年3月

我想那些购买苹果的人，一定有不一样的思考模式，他们是这个世界上最具有创新精神的人。那些人他们出门不是去找一份工作，而是去改变世界。并且他们使用任何他们可能获得的绝妙工具去改变世界。我们就是在为这些人制造工具。

乔布斯回归苹果的演讲，1997年

招聘新人进来可没有那么简单。新人进入公司之后，需要给他们营造一个环境，让他们感觉周围都是一些和自己水平旗鼓相当的人才，他们的工作是要成就一番大事的，让他们感到他们的工作会带来巨大的而影响，是那个强大的、清晰的"愿景"的一部分。招聘这事儿一个人单枪匹马可做不来，所以我发现协同招聘以及招收"明星球员"才是最好的办法。任何一个面试者都要和最少一打来自不同部门的面试官交谈 —— 不仅仅是他要去的那个部门的面试官，这样一来，不仅你的"明星球员"和全公司都有了广泛接触 —— 如果他们能够在这个过程中强烈感受到企业文化，就会给他们以信心 —— 但也可以随时被任何一个面试官否决掉。

《巨人公司》，1997年

What's reinvigorating this company is two things: One, there's a lot of really talented people in this company who listened to the world tell them they were losers for a couple of years, and some of them were on the verge of starting to believe it themselves. But they're not losers. What they didn't have was a good set of coaches, a good plan. A good senior management team. But they have that now.

Business Week, May 25, 1998

At Apple we gave all our employees stock options very early on. We were among the first in Silicon Valley to do that. And when I returned, I took away most of the cash bonuses and replaced them with options. No cars, no planes, no bonuses. Basically, everybody gets a salary and stock…It's a very egalitarian way to run a company that Hewlett-Packard pioneered and that Apple, I would like to think, helped establish.

CNNMoney / Fortune, November 9, 1998

Here's to the crazy ones, the misfits, the rebels, the troublemakers, the round pegs in the square holes, the ones who see things differently. They're not fond of rules. And they have no respect for the status quo. You can quote them, disagree with them, glorify or vilify them. About the only thing you can't do is ignore them, because they change things. They push the human race forward.

Apple's "Think Different" commercial, 1997

挽救这个公司的是两个因素：一是公司里有很多真正富有天赋的人才，多年来，这些天才员工一直听到外界说他们是失败者，其中有些人连自己也快要相信了。但是，他们不是失败者。他们欠缺的是好的教练、好的计划。二是拥有优秀的管理团队。现在，他们终于有了。

《商业周刊》杂志，1998年5月25日

在苹果公司，我们从一开始就把股票期权分给了员工。我们是第一家在硅谷，做到这一点的公司。我回到苹果之后，取消了大部分的现金奖励，而用期权代替。没有汽车、没有飞机、没有奖金。基本上，每个人都能拿到薪水和股票……这种非常平等的运作公司的方式是由惠普开创的，而苹果进一步巩固了这种方式。

美国有线电视新闻网财经频道/《财富》杂志，1998年11月9日

向那些疯狂的家伙们致敬，他们特立独行，他们桀骜不驯，他们惹是生非，他们格格不入，他们用与众不同的眼光看待事物，他们不喜欢墨守成规，他们也不愿安于现状。你可以引用他们，反对他们，质疑他们，颂扬或是诋毁他们，但唯独不能漠视他们。因为他们改变了事物。他们推动人类向前发展。

1997年苹果Think Different电视广告

While some may see them as the crazy ones, we see genius. Because the people who are crazy enough to think they can change the world, are the ones who do.

Apple's "Think Different" commercial, 1997

I almost forgot. We're profitable.

MacWorld, January 1998

有时候人们会认为他们太疯狂，然而我们却看到了他们的影响力，因为只有疯狂到认为自己有能力改变世界的人，才能真正地改变世界。

我差点忘了告诉你们了，苹果公司又开始盈利了。

1997 年苹果 Think Different 电视广告

苹果展销会，1998 年 1 月

7. 奋斗
Strive

2006年9月12日，乔布
斯推出新款iPod

Jobs brings the new
iPod out, September 12,
2006

2002年7月，美国纽约，苹果创始人史蒂夫·乔布斯在曼哈顿出席一家苹果商店的开幕仪式

Steve Jobs, the founder of Apple, attends a Apple store's opening ceremony in Manhattan, July 2002

2010年6月7日，美国
加利福尼亚州旧金山，
苹果公司首席执行官乔
布斯在一年一度的苹果
全球开发者大会上发布
iPhone4

Apple's CEO Jobs
launchs iPhone4
at World Wide
Developers Conference
in San Francisco
Calafornia,June 7,2010

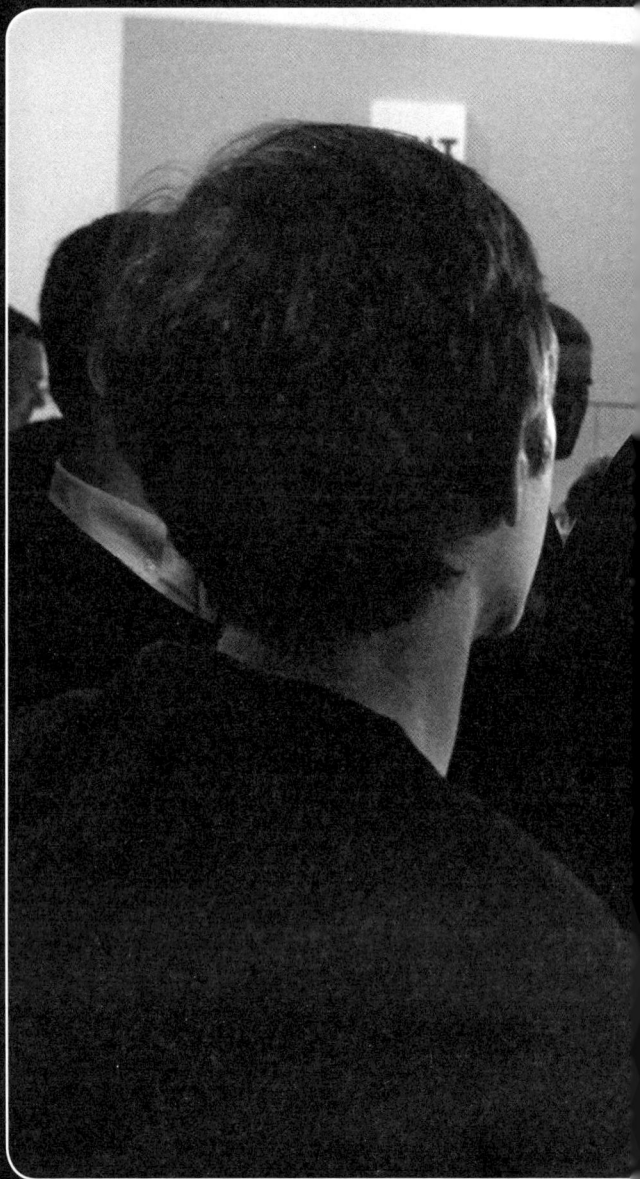

What I found when I go there was a zillion and one products. It was amazing. And I started to ask people, now why would I recommend a 3400 over a 4400? When should somebody jump up to a 6500, but not a 7300? And after three weeks, I couldn't figure this out. If I couldn't figure this out…how could our customers figure this out?

Apple Worldwide Developers Conference,1998

We've reviewed the road map of new products and axed more than 70 percent of them, keeping the30 percent that were gems. The product teams at Apple are very excited. There's SO much low-hanging fruit, it's easy to turn around.

Macworld Expo,January6, 1998

That's been one of my mantras—focus and simplicity. Simple can be harder than complex: You have to work hard to get your thinking clean to make it simple. But it's worth it in the end because once you get there, you can move mountains.

Business Week,
May 25, 1998

I'd never been so tired in my life. I'd come home at about ten o'clock at night and flop straight into bed, then haul myself out at six the next morning and take a shower and go to work. My wife deserves all the credit for keeping me at it. She supported me and kept the family together with a husband in absentia.

CNNMoney / Fortune,
November 9, 1998

我接任苹果公司的时候，看到的是数目繁多的产品。这太不可思议了。于是我开始问公司员工，为什么推荐3400而非4400？为什么直接跳到6500，而非7300？三个星期后，我依然无法弄清楚到底是为什么。如果连我都无法弄懂这一点的话，我们的顾客怎么可能弄清楚？

我们重新审查了一遍新产品的路线图，砍掉了70%，留下的30%是真正有价值的部分。苹果的产品团队非常兴奋，这些都是唾手可得的果实，想变得越来越好很容易。

我的秘诀就是 —— 专注和简单。简单比复杂更难，你必须努力让你的想法变得清晰明了，让它变得简单。但是，到最后，你会发现它值得你去做。因为一旦你做到了简单，你就能搬动大山。

我这辈子没这么累过。我每天晚上十点到家之后，就直挺挺地倒在床上昏睡过去，第二天早上六点钟挣扎起床，洗个澡就去上班。辛苦了我的太太，让我能撑了过来。她不仅全力支持我，还在丈夫失踪的情况下，把家一切打理得妥妥当当。

苹果电脑全球研发者大会，1998年

麦金塔世界博览会，1998年1月6日

《商业周刊》杂志，1998年5月25日

美国有线电视新闻网财经频道/《财富》杂志，1998年11月9日

For something this complicated, it's really hard to design products by focus groups. A lot of times, people don't know what they want until you show it to them.

Business Week,
May 25, 1998

"In most people's vocabularies, design means veneer, But to me, nothing could be further from the meaning of design. Design is the fundamental soul of a man-made creation that ends up expressing itself in successive outer layers.

Fortune

I've never believed that they're separate. Leonardo da Vinci was a great artist and a great scientist. Michelangelo knew a tremendous amount about how to cut stone at the quarry. The finest dozen computer scientists I know are all musicians. Some are better than others, but they all consider that an important part of their life. I don't believe that the best people in any of these fields see themselves as one branch of a forked tree. I just don't see that. People bring these things together a lot. Dr. Land at Polaroid said, "I want Polaroid to stand at the intersection of art and science, "and I've never forgotten that. I think that that's possible, and I think a lot of people have tried.

Time, October 10,1999

对于如此复杂的东西，以讨论小组的形式来设计产品就很困难。很多时候，人们并不清楚他们需要什么，直到你把产品展示给他们看。

《商业周刊》杂志，
1998年5月25日

在大多数人看来，设计就和镶嵌工艺差不多，但是对于我而言，"设计"一次绝无任何引申含义。设计是一个人工作品的核心灵魂，并最终由外壳表达出来。

《财富》杂志

我从不相信他们是互不相关的。列奥纳多·达·芬奇既是个伟大的艺术是家，同时也是伟大的科学家。米开朗基罗知道如何在采石场雕琢石块。我也知道很多最优秀的电脑科学家都是音乐家，他们都把这个当做生活中的重要部分，我不相信这些领域中的杰出人才们会把自己只看成一颗布满枝杈的树上其中一个枝条，反正我还没有见过，他们总是把这些东西结合在一起。宝丽来公司的兰德博士说过："我希望宝丽来能把艺术和科学结合在一起。"这句话我一直印象深刻。我认为实现这点，完全有可能，而且有很多人正在为此努力着。

《时代》杂志，
1999年10月10日

The roots of Apple were to build computers for people, not for corporations. The world doesn't need another Dell or Compaq.

Time, October 18, 1999

The cure for Apple is not cost-cutting. The cure for Apple is to innovate its way out of its current predicament.

Apple Confidential: The Real Story of Apple Computer Inc, May 1999

That doesn't mean we don't listen to customers, but it's hard for them to tell you what they want when they've never seen anything remotely like it. Take desktop video editing. I never got one request from someone who wanted to edit movies on his computer. Yet now that people see it, they say, "Oh my God, that's great!"

Fortune, January 24, 2000

When these people sell out, even though they get fabulously rich, they're gypping themselves out of one of the potentially most rewarding experiences of their unfolding lives. Without it, they may never know their values or how to keep their newfound wealth in perspective.

Fortune, January 24, 2000

苹果的根本宗旨是要生产给普通人用的，而非给公司用的电脑。这世界没必要再出来一个戴尔或者康柏了。

《时代》杂志，1999年10月18日

治疗苹果的良方不是削减成本，而是不断地推陈出新，走出当前的困境。

《苹果机密：苹果电脑的真实故事》，1999年5月

这并不是说，我们不倾听消费者的意见，而是当他们还没有见过这么先进的东西的时候，你就要他们告诉你他们想要什么，这简直太难了。就拿桌面视频编辑软件来说吧，从来没有一个人向我提出要求，想在他的电脑上编辑电影。但是现在，当人们看到这款产品时，他们惊呼，"天呐，这简直太神奇了！"

《财富》杂志，2000年1月24日

当这些人将他们创办的公司出售时，尽管他们获得了极大的财富，但是他们可能失去了人生中最为宝贵的经验。没有这种经验，他们可能就永远不知道他们的价值，或者永远不知道如何正确地保有他们创造的财富。

《财富》杂志，2000年1月24日

I'm always keeping my eyes open for the next big opportunity, but the way the world is now, it will take enormous resources, both in money and in engineering talent, to make it happen. I don't know what that next big thing might be, but I have a few ideas.

CNNMoney January 24. 2000

I hope that we've been able to prove to our shareholders at Pixar and our shareholders at Apple that maybe we could pull this dual CEO thing off. So I'm not going to any of my duties at Pixar or at Apple. But I am pleased to announce today that I'm going to drop the "interim" title.

MacWorld,2000

I get to come to work every day and work with the most talented people on the planet, at Apple and Pixar. But these jobs are team sports. I accept your thanks on behalf of everybody at Apple.

MacWorld,2000

The problem with the Internet startup craze isn't that too many people are starting companies; it's that too many people aren't sticking with it. That's somewhat understandable, because there are many moments that are filled with despair and agony, when you have to fire people and cancel things and deal with very difficult situations. That's when you find out who you are and what your values are.

Fortune, January24, 2000

对即将到来的良机，我总是睁大双眼，不会错失，但如今的世界，要想获得机遇，必须拥有众多资源 —— 无论是金钱还是技术人才。下一个大事件是什么，我不知道，我有的，只是一些创意。

美国有线电视新闻网财经频道，2000 年 1 月 24 日

我希望我能向皮克斯公司的股民和苹果公司的股民证明，我这个有着双重身份的首席执行官能为他们做好每一件事。因此，我还会继续在皮克斯公司和苹果公司工作。今天我很高兴地向你们宣布，我要放弃"临时"首席执行官的头衔了。

MacWorld，2000 年

我每天都和世界上最聪明的人们一起工作，无论是在苹果还是在皮克斯。但是这些成就就是团队合作的结果。我代表苹果公司的每一个人，接受你们的感谢。

MacWorld，2000 年

互联网创业热的问题不是有太多人开始创办公司，而是有太多人不能坚持到底。这一点似乎可以理解，因为在创业过程中有很多时候充满了绝望和苦恼，尤其当你在解雇员工、取消计划和应付艰难局面的时候。但是，这正是你展现自己是谁，你的价值是什么的时候。

《财富》杂志，2000 年 1 月 24 日

We made the buttons on the screen look so good you'll want to lick them.

On Mac OS X, *Fortune*, January24, 2000

We've gone through the operating system and looked at everything and asked how can we simplify this and make it more powerful at the same time.

ABC News, Jobs on Mac OS X Beta

This is what customers pay us for--to sweat all these details so it's easy and pleasant for them to use our computers. We're supposed to be really good at this.

Fortune, January 24, 2000

This transformation's going to make some people uneasy--people from the PC world, like you and me. It's going to make US uneasy because the PC has taken US a long way—it's brilliant. And we like to talk about the post-PC era, but when it really starts to happen, I think it's uncomfortable for a lot of people.

D8 Conference,June1-3, 2010

我们把屏幕上的按键设计得如此完美，就是为了让你情不自禁地点击它们。

《财富》杂志，2000年1月24日，乔布斯谈 Mac OS X 操作系统

我们开发操作系统，注重每个细节，并思考在保证产品功能强大的同时，如何简化它。

美国广播公司新闻，乔布斯谈 Mac OS X 操作系统

这就是消费者付钱购买的东西 —— 你在所有这些细节上的流汗努力就是为了让消费者使用我们的电脑时感到更轻松和惬意。我们应该真正地精通此道。

《财富》杂志，
2000年1月24日

这次变革会让有些人感到焦虑 —— 像你我这样来自 pc 世界的人。我们之所以会觉得不适，是因为 pc 机陪伴我们走过了这么长的时间，那是卓越而美好的时代。我们愿意谈论后 PC 时代，但一旦真的到来到了，很多人都会觉得难以适应。

D8大会
2000年6月1-3日

You can't imagine how many people think we're crazy for not doing a Palm, I won't lie; we thought about that a lot. But I started asking myself, how useful are they, really? how many people at a given meeting show up with one? Whether I was here or at Disney or at Pixar, the percentage peaked about a year ago at 50 percent, and it's now dwindled to less than 10 percent. It kind of went up really fast and then went down.

Fortune,2001

Join the music revolution with iTunes, and make your music devices ten times more valuable.

New Products Promotion Conference, January 2001

This amazing little device holds a thousand songs, and it goes right in my pocket.

New Products Promotion Conference, January 2001

We believe that 80% of the people stealing stuff don't want to be, there's just no legal alternative, So we said, 'Let's create a legal alternative to this.' Everybody wins. Music companies win. The artists win. Apple wins. And the user wins, because he gets a better service and doesn't have to be a thief.

Esquire

你们可能想想不到有多少人认为我们不研发牛顿掌上电脑简直就是一种不可思议的做法。在这里我不撒谎，有很多人都有这种想法。但我也一直在反思，掌上电脑真的有用吗？现在在一个会场上，究竟有多少人手里拿着一个掌上电脑呢？不论在这里还是在迪士尼公司，或者皮克斯公司，据我所知，使用这种电脑的人在一年前曾达到50%，但现在已经减少到不足10%了。这种掌上电脑的兴盛和衰败都是非常迅速的。

《财富》杂志，2001年

和iTunes一起加入音乐革命吧，它可以把你的音乐设备的价值增加十倍。

苹果新产品发布会，2001年1月

这绝妙的小机器里装着1000首歌曲，而且刚好能放进我的口袋。

苹果新产品发布会，2001年10月

我们相信，有80%下载盗版的人都是不得已的，只是没有给他们提供合法的选择而已。所以我们说："我们创立一个合法的途径吧。"这样大家都会受益。音乐公司能盈利，艺术家能盈利，苹果公司也能盈利，而用户也会有所收获，因为他们既享受到了更好的服务，又不必偷窃。

《君子》杂志

I would trade all of my technology for an afternoon with Socrates.

News Week, 2001

We believe the next great era is for the personal computer to be the digital hub of all these devices.

Time, January14, 2002

I think it's brought the a lot closer together, and will continue to do that. There are downsides to everything; there are unintended consequences to everything. The most corrosive piece of technology that I've ever seen is called television — but then, again, television, at its best, is magnificent.

Rolling Stone, December 3, 2003

But it's a disservice to constantly put things in this radical new light — that it's going to change everything. Things don't have to change the world to be important.

Wired, February 1996

Most people make the mistake of thinking design is what it looks like. That's not what we think design is. It's not just what it looks like and feels like. Design is how it works.

New York Times, 2003

I understand the appeal of a slow burn, but personally I'm a big-bang guy.

Harvard Business School, *Working Knowledge for Business Leaders*, June 16,2003

我愿意把我所有的科技去换取和苏格拉底相处的一个下午。

《新闻周刊》，2001 年

我们相信，下一个伟大的时代，是个人电脑成为所有这些设备的数字中枢的时代。

《时代》杂志，
2002 年 1 月 14 日

无论是现在还是将来，技术都能够让全世界的人获得更加紧密的联系。任何事物都有它的弊端，都会带来意想不到的后果。我见过的最有害的技术就是电视机，但是，从好的方面来说，电视又是最了不起的发明。

《滚石》杂志，
2003 年 12 月 3 日

但是，我们不能以一种偏激的态度来看待这些技术，认为技术能够改变一切。如果这样想的话，就很危险。因为技术不一定要改变世界才能显示出它的重要性。

《连线》杂志，1996 年 2 月

大多数人误以为设计就是看上去如何，我们不这么认为，设计并非体现在外表和感觉上，而是体验起来如何！

《纽约时报》，2003 年

我明白慢热不错，但就我自己而言，我就是一个火爆脾气的家伙。

哈佛商学院，
《给商界领袖的工作知识》，
2003 年 6 月 16 日

The system is that there is no system. That doesn't mean we don't have process. Apple is a very disciplined company, and we have great processes. But that's not what it's about. Process makes you more efficient.

Business Week, October12, 2004

We designed iMac to deliver the things consumers care about most—the excitement of the Internet and the simplicity of the Mac. iMac is next year's computer for$1, 299, not last year's computer for $999.

Apple Confidential 2. 0, 2004

It will go down in history as a turning point for the music industry. This is landmark stuff. I can't overestimate it!

On the iTunes Music Store, *Fortune*, May 12, 2003

Apple's in a pretty interesting position. Because, as you may know, almost every song and CD is made on a Mac—it's recorded on a Mac; it's mixed on a Mac. The artwork's done on a Mac. Almost every artist I've met has an iPod, and most of the music execs now have iPods.

Rolling Stone, December 3, 2003

系统就是没有系统。这并不是说我们没有工作流程。苹果是一家非常规范的公司，我们拥有伟大的工作流程。但是，这不是问题的全部。工作流程只是为了让你的工作效率更高。

《商业周刊》杂志，
2004年10月12日

我们设计iMac是为了提供消费者最关心的东西 —— 令人兴奋的互联网和简单的Mac标价1,299美元的iMac是明年的电脑，而999美元的是去年的电脑。

《苹果机密2.0》，2004年

它将成为音乐行业发展历程中的一个重要的转折点。它就是标志性的东西。我一点也没有夸大其词。

《财富》杂志，2003年5月
12日，乔布斯谈论iTunes
音乐商店

苹果公司处在一个非常有趣的位置。因为，你可能知道，几乎每首歌曲和CD歌曲都是用Mac制作的；歌曲在Mac电脑上进行混音。在Mac电脑上完成艺术品制作。几乎每一个我见过的艺术家都有一个iPod，且大多数音乐人拥有iPod。

《滚石》杂志，
2003年12月3日

It's because when you buy our products, and three months later you get stuck on something, you quickly figure out[how to get past it]. And you think, "Wow, someone over there at Apple actually thought of this!"…There's almost no product in the world that you have that experience with, but you have it with a Mac. And you have it with an iPod.

Bloomberg Businessweek,
October 12, 2004

Innovation comes from people meeting up in the hallways or calling each other at 10:30 at night with a new idea, or because they realized something that shoots holes in how we've been thinking about a problem. It's ad hoc meetings of six people called by someone who thinks he has figured out the coolest new thing ever and who wants to know what other people think of his idea.

Business Week,
October12, 2004

And it comes from saying no to 1,000 things to make sure we don't get on the wrong track or try to do too much. We're always thinking about new markets we could enter, but it's only by saying no that you can concentrate on the things that are really important.

Business Week,
October12, 2004

人们常常问我说为什么苹果的顾客会如此忠实。当然不是因为他们是什么苹果教会的信徒，这些都是无稽之谈。

顾客之所以会忠实于苹果，是因为如果你购买了苹果产品，用了三个月，发现被一个问题给卡住了，但马上又找到了解决的办法，这时你就会想，"啊，原来苹果公司的人竟然也想到了同样的问题！"除了苹果之外，世界上大概再找不到什么产品能然你有这样的使用体验了吧。这种感觉，苹果电脑能给你，一台 iPod 也能给你。

《彭博商业周刊》杂志，2004 年 10 月 12 日

创新来自于人们在走廊上的交流，或在夜里 10：30 的电话，或他们意识到自己思维方式的漏洞。创新来自于某个人临时召集的六人会议，这个人认为自己明白了世界上最酷最新的事物，而且想知道其他人如何看待他的创意。

《商业周刊》杂志，2004 年 10 月 12 日

创意来自于我们对 1000 种东西说不，从而确保我们不会误入歧途或陷入太多琐碎的事务。我们总是在思考我们能够进入的新市场，但是只有学会拒绝，你才能集中精力关注真正重要的事情。

《商业周刊》杂志，2004 年 10 月 12 日

Sometimes when you innovate, you make mistakes. It is best to admit them quickly, and get on with improving your other innovations.

The Journey is the Reward

What happened was, the designers came up with this really great idea. Then they take it to the engineers, and the engineers go, "Nah, we can't do that. That's impossible. "And so it gets a lot worse. Then they take it to the manufacturing people, and they go, "We can't build that!"And it gets alot worse... Sure enough, when we took it to the engineers, they said, "Oh. "And they came up with 38 reasons. And I said, "No, no, we're doing this. "And they said, "Well, why?"And I said, "Because I'm the CEO and I think it can be done. "And so they kind of begrudgingly did it. But then it was a big hit. "

*Time,*October 16, 2005

We never talk about future products. There used to be a saying at Apple: Isn't it funny?A ship that leaks from the top. So—I don't wanna perpetuate that. So I really can't say.

ABCNews. com,June 29,2005

I've always wanted to own and control the primary technology in everything we do.

Business Week, October12, 2004

在创新的过程中，你可能会犯错误，最好马上承认，并在接下来的行事中加以改进。

《苹果电脑成功之旅》

事情是这样的，设计师们提出了这个绝妙的想法，然后告诉了工程师，可工程师说："不，我们做不了这个，这根本不可能实现。"这可真糟糕，于是他们又找到了制造工人，可制造工人说："我们做不出来！"一次比一次更糟糕……果然，当我们带着他去找了工程师，他们说："啊？"然后提出了38条不做的理由，于是我说，"不，不，我们做的就是这个。"他们又说，"那么，是为什么呢？"我说，"因为我是CEO，我觉得这事儿能做成。"尽管最后他们做得很勉强，但这已经算很成功了。

《时代》杂志，
2005年10月16日

我们从不谈论未来的产品是什么样子的。苹果公司里流传着一句话：一艘船居然从顶上开始漏了，很好笑吧。所以 —— 我不想让这句话一直不断成为现实，所以我真的不能说。

ABCNews.com,
2005年6月29日

我一直想拥有和控制我们所有产品的主要技术。

《商业周刊》杂志，
2004年10月12日

We're the only company that owns the whole widget—the hardware, the software and the operating system, We can take full responsibility for the user experience. We can do things that the other guys can't do.

Time

Pretty much, Apple and Dell are the only ones in this industry making money. They make it by being Wal—Mart. We make it by innovation.

Macworld, 2004

Apple's market share is bigger than BMW's or Mercedes's or Porsche's in the automotive market. What's wrong with being BMW or Mercedes?

Macworld, 2004

The place where Apple has been standing for the last two decades is exactly where computer technology and the consumer electronics markets are converging. So it's not like we're having to CROSS the river to go somewhere else: the other side of the river coming to us.

CNNMoney / Fortune, February 21, 2005

我们是唯一一家掌握全部设备的公司——硬件、软件、操作系统。我们能够为用户体验负全部的责任。我们能够做到其他公司做不到的事情。

《时代》杂志

整个电脑产业赚钱的只有苹果和戴尔，不同的是，他们靠的是成为电脑界的沃尔玛，我们靠的是创新。

Macworld，2004 年

我们的市场份额比宝马、奔驰或保时捷在汽车行业的份额都要高。没有人会因为宝马和奔驰的份额低而质疑他们。

Macworld，2004 年

苹果在近20年所代表的正是电脑技术和消费电子市场的融合。所以，并不是我们必须要跨过这条河，而是河对岸自己过来了。

美国有线电视新闻网财经频道/《财富》杂志，2005 年 2 月 21

I had a scan at 7:30 in the morning, and it clearly showed a tumor on my pancreas. I didn't even know what a pancreas was. The doctors told me this was almost certainly a type of cancer that is incurable, and that I should expect to live no longer than three to six months. My doctor advised me to go home and get my affairs in order, which is doctor's code for prepare to die. It means to try to tell your kids everything you thought you'd have the next 10 years to tell them in just a few months. It means to make sure everything is buttoned up so that it will be as easy as possible for your family. It means to say your goodbyes.

Stanford Commencement Speech, June 2005

I lived with that diagnosis all day. Later that evening I had a biopsy, where they stuck an endoscope down my throat, through my stomach and into my intestines, put a needle into my pancreas and got a few cells from the tumor. I was sedated, but my wife, who was there, told me that when they viewed the cells under a microscope the doctors started crying because it turned out to be a very rare form of pancreatic cancer that is curable with surgery.

Stanford Commencement Speech, June 2005

我在早晨七点半做了一个检查，检查清楚的显示在我的胰腺有一个肿瘤。我当时都不知道胰腺是什么东西。医生告诉我那很可能是一种无法治愈的癌症，我还有三到六个月的时间活在这个世界上。我的医生叫我回家，然后整理好我的一切，那就是医生准备死亡的程序。那意味着你将要把未来十年对你小孩说的话在几个月里面说完；那意味着把每件事情都搞定，让你的家人会尽可能轻松的生活；那意味着你要说"再见了"。

斯坦福毕业典礼演讲，
2005 年 6 月

我整天和那个诊断书一起生活。后来有一天早上我作了一个活切片检查，医生将一个内窥镜从我的喉咙伸进去，通过我的胃，然后进入我的肠子，用一根针在我的胰腺上的肿瘤上取了几个细胞。我当时很镇静，因为我被注射了镇静剂。但是我的妻子在那里，后来告诉我，当医生在显微镜地下观察这些细胞的时候他们开始尖叫，因为这些细胞最后竟然是一种非常罕见的可以用手术治愈的胰腺癌症。

斯坦福毕业典礼演讲，
2005 年 6 月

This weekend I underwent a successful surgery to remove a cancerous tumor from my pancreas... I will not require any chemotherapy or radiation treatments... I will be recuperating during the month of August, and expect to return to work in September. While I'm out, I've asked Tim Cook to be responsible for Apple's day to day operations, so we shouldn't miss a beat.

E-mail from Steve Jobs, August 1, 2004

Most of us can't wait to get to work in the morning. But it's not like Apple has somehow morphed into a mass-market consumer electronics company. Our DNA hasn't changed. It's that mass-market consumer electronics is turning into Apple.

CNNMoney / Fortune, February 21, 2005

You or I move into a new house, and the first thing we do is call the phone company to get our land line turned on. Kids, they just move in with their cell phones. Stereos are the same: kids aren't getting stereos; they're getting speakers for their iPods. That's become the audio market. People are buying iPods and Bose speakers instead of a JVC or Sony stereo system.

MacWorld, 2005

在这个周末我在医院做了一个成功的手术，医生把我胰脏上的恶性肿瘤切除了……另外，我已不再需要接受任何化疗和放疗了……我会在8月份里静心休养，预计在9月份就会重返工作岗位。我已经要求副总裁蒂姆·库克负责苹果公司的日常事务了，因为苹果公司不能"一日无主"。

乔布斯的邮件，
2004年8月1日

我们大多数人每天早上都迫不及待的来公司上班。但这并不代表苹果在一定程度上已经转变成了一个面向大众消费电子市场的公司，或者我们的DNA改变了，不是。而是大众消费电子市场转向了苹果。

美国有线电视新闻网财经
频道/《财富》杂志，
2005年2月21日

当我们搬进一所新房子的时候，我们要做的第一件事就是请电话公司给我们装上电话线，然后把电话开通。而孩子们就不用了，他们只需要把手机打进来就可以了。立体声音响也是一样：孩子们只需使用iPod播放器就行了。这样就形成了立体声播放器市场。人们宁愿去购买iPod播放器和博士音响，也不愿购买日本胜利公司或索尼公司的大型立体声音响系统。

MacWorld，2005年

It's insane: We all have busy lives, we have jobs, we have interests, and some of US have children. Everyone's lives are just getting busier,not less busy,in this busy society. You just don't have time to learn this stuff,and everything's getting more complicated...We both don't have a lot of time to learn how to use a washing machine or a phone.

*The Independent,*October 29,2005

In the last quarter I am pleased to report that we have sold over four and a half million iPods. That in a 50 percent growth year over year. We have sold over 10 million iPods to date and over 8 million of them in 2004. the digital music era is upon us, and we are leading the charge.

MacWorld, 2005

Music companies make more money when they sell a song on than when they sell a CD. If they want to raise prices, it's because they're greedy. If the price goes up, people turn back to piracy, and everybody loses.

Guardian, September 22, 2005

真是太疯狂了：我们整日生活得忙碌不堪，我们有工作，我们有爱好，有的人还有孩子。在这个忙碌的社会中，每个人的日子只会是越过越忙，不会越来越清闲。你没时间去学东西，一切变得越来越复杂……我们都没有时间去学习怎样使用一台洗衣机或一部电话。

《独立报》，
2005年10月29日

在上一年的最后一个季度里，我很高兴地告诉大家，我们已经销售出去了450万台iPod播放器。我们iPod播放器销售量每年仍递增50%。到此为止，我们销售的iPod播放器的数量达到了1000多万台，进2004年一年销售量就有800万台。是我们引领了整个数字化音乐时代的潮流。

MacWorld，2005年

音乐公司们靠iTunes卖歌赚的钱比卖CD赚得还多，如果他们想涨价，这就是贪得无厌。如果价格高了，人们又该去找盗版来听了——这样就都输了。

《卫报》，2005年9月22日

We had the hardware experience, the industrial design expertise and the software expertise, including iTunes. One of the biggest insights we had was that we decided not to try to manage your music library on the iPod, but to manage it in iTunes. Other companies tried to do everything on the device itself and made it so complicated that it was useless.

Newsweek, October 16,2006

Look at the design of a lot of consumer products--they're really complicated surfaces. We tried to make something much more holistic and simple. When you first start off trying to solve a problem, the first solutions you come up with are very complex, and most people stop there. But if you keep going, and live with the problem and peel more layers of the onion off, you can oftentimes arrive at some very elegant and simple solutions. Most people just don't put in the time or energy to get there. We believe that customers are smart and want objects which are well thought through.

Newsweek, October 16,2006

We're going to get a chance to continue to work with Disney, but rather than two companies with two sets of shareholders and different agendas, we're just going to be one company where we can all focus on making the best films in the world and, you know, distributing theme and getting also the characters into Disney's unique assets like their theme parks, et cetera.

CNN interview in 2006

我们有硬件经验，掌握工业设计技术和软件技术 —— 包括 iTunes。我们最具前瞻性的观点就在于我们没有想方设法地把音乐图书馆放到你的 iPod 里，而是把它设计到了 iTunes 中去。其他公司总是想把所有东西都塞进设备里面，导致产品太过复杂，反而变得失去了用处。

《新闻周刊》，
2006 年 10 月 16 日

看看现在那么多消费品的设计吧，外观一个比一个复杂。我们想要做的，是整体性更强，更加简约的东西。当你开始解决一个问题的时候，你最先想出的方案总是非常复杂的，大多数人就此止步不前了。但是，如果你继续向前探索，像剥洋葱一样一层一层地拨开笼罩这个问题的迷雾，你就可能会找到一些非常简单完美的解决方案。大多数人不愿意投入时间或精力来找到这个方案。我们相信，消费者的眼睛是雪亮的，他们只会购买经过深思熟虑的产品。

《新闻周刊》杂志，
2006 年 10 月 16

我们有幸继续与迪士尼共事，但如今已不再呈两家公司，两组股东班子和不同的业务规划，我们会是一家公司，专注于制作和发行全世界最好看的电影，而且让皮克斯创造的角色融入迪士尼的独有资产中去，如主题公园，等等。

美国有线电视新闻网采访，
2006 年

The people who go to see our movies are trusting US with something very important--their time and their imagination. So in order to respect that trust, we have to keep changing; we have to challenge ourselves and try to surprise our audiences with something new every time.

To Infinity and Beyond 2007

We've pioneered the whole medium of computer animation, but John[Lasseter]once said--and this really stuck with me—"No amount of technology will turn a bad story into a good story,"...That dedication to quality is really ingrained in the culture of this studio.

To Infinity and Beyond 2007

Pixar's seen by a lot of folks as an overnight success, but if you really look closely, most over night successes took a long time.

To Infinity and Beyond 2007

I think if you do something and it turns out pretty good, then you should go do something else wonderful, not dwell on it for too long. Just figure out what's next.

NBC Nightly News,
May 2006

170

看我们电影的人都是因为对我们的信任，因为这份信任，他们把很重要的两件东西托付给了我们 —— 金钱和想象力。为了不辜负这份信任，我们必须要不断改变，我们必须不断挑战自我，努力做到每一次都用新鲜的东西给观众带来惊喜。

《超越无限》，2007 年

我们是电脑动画制作工具的开创先锋，但约翰·拉塞特曾经说过一句话，让我感触颇深 —— "再好的技术，也没办法把烂故事变成好故事，"……对故事质量重视的思想已经深植于我们工作室的文化当中。

《超越无限》，2007 年

在很多人看来，皮克斯公司似乎是一夜成名，但如果你仔细观察，会发现所谓的"一夜成名"需要很长的时间。

《超越无限》，2007 年

如果你做某件事情，结果非常好，你就应该尝试做些其他有意义的事情，不要在一件事情上逗留太久。要经常想想下一步做什么。

《NBC 夜间新闻》，2006 年 5 月

When you first start off trying to solve a problem, the first solutions you come up with are very complex, and most people stop there. But if you keep going, and live with the problem and peel more layers of the onion off, you can often times arrive at some very elegant and simple solutions. Most people just don't put in the time or energy to get there. We believe that customers are smart, and want objects which are well thought through.

MSNBC and *News Week interview*, October14, 2006

We make tools for people. Tools to create, tools to communicate. The age we're living in, these tools surprise you…That's why I love what we do. Because we make these tools, and we're constantly surprised with what people do with them.

Ds Conference: All Things Digital,2007

All we are is our ideas, or people. That's what keeps us going to work in the morning, to hang around these great bright people. I've always thought that recruiting is the heart and soul of what we do.

DS Conference: All Things Digital, May 30,2007

Let's go invent tomorrow rather than worrying about what happened yesterday.

Ds Conference: All Things Digital,May30,2007

当你开始解决一个问题的时候，你最先想出的方案总是非常复杂的，大多数人就此止步不前了。但是，如果你继续向前探索，像剥洋葱一样一层一层地拨开笼罩这个问题的迷雾，你就可能会找到一些非常简单完美的解决方案。大多数人不愿意投入时间或精力来找到这个方案。我们相信，消费者的眼睛是雪亮的，他们只会购买经过深思熟虑的产品。

美国 MSNBC 网站和《新闻周刊》杂志采访，
2006 年 10 月 14 日

我们为人们制造的工具，是用来进行创造的工具，是用来进行交流的工具。在我们生活的这个时代，这些工具给你带来了惊喜……这也是我热爱我的工作的原因所在。因为我们制造这些工具，我们常常看到，人们因为利用这些工具做的事情而感到和我们同样的惊喜。

D5 大会：彻底数字化，
2007 年

我们自己就是我们的想法。正是这个思想支撑着我们每天早起上班，环绕在那些伟大的聪明人士周围，我一直认为为公司补充新鲜血液是我们工作的中心和灵魂。

D5 大会：彻底数字化，2007
年 5 月 30 日

我们应该去放手创造明天，而不是为了昨天懊悔。

D5 大会：彻底数字化，2007
年 5 月 30 日

173

People say you have to have a lot of passion for what you're doing and it's totally true. And the reason is because it's so hard that if you don't, any rational person would give up. It's really hard. And you have to do it over a sustained period of time. So if you don't love it, if you're not having fun doing it, you don't really love it, you're going to give up. And that's what happens to most people, actually. If you really look at the ones that ended up being"successful"in the eyes of the society and the ones that didn't, oftentimes it's the ones[who] were successful loved what they did, So they could persevere when it got really tough. And the ones that didn't love it quit because they're sane, right?Who would want to put up with this stuff if you don't love it?So it's a lot of hard work and it's a lot of worrying constantly and if you don't love it, you're going to fail.

D5 Conference: All Things Digital,May30,2007

At Apple, there are ten really important decisions to make every week. It's a transactional company; it's got a lot of new products every month. And if some of those decisions are wrong, maybe you can fix them a few months later. At Pixar because I'm not directing the movies, there are just a few really important strategic decisions to make every month, maybe even every quarter, but they're really hard to change. Pixar's much slower paced, but you can't change your mind when you go down these paths.

To Infinity and Beyond 2007

人们总说，你要对你的工作满怀热情，这话一点不错，毫无激情的去干一件事情会让人非常难受，任何一个有理性的人都受不了。如果你要在一段时间内持续的去做一件事情，如果你不爱它，如果你不能从中找到乐趣，你早晚会半途而废的。实际上，这样的情况大多数人都遇到过。如果你看见某人最后终于取得了成功 —— 被整个社会和那些不成功的人认可的成功，究其原因，通常是因为他们成功的爱上了自己做的事情，所以即便是在最艰苦的时候他们也坚持了下来。而那些不爱它的人中途放弃的原因是因为他们是神志清醒的，对吗？如果不爱它，谁又会容忍它；如果你不爱他，随之而来的时诸多困难和忧虑；如果你不爱它，等待你的是失败的结果。

D5大会：彻底数字化，2007年5月30日

在苹果公司，每周都要做出10个非常重要的决策，苹果是个处理事务型的公司，每个月不会有太多的新产品要发布，如果哪个决策做错了，可能几个月之后就能修正过来；而在皮克斯公司，因为我不是电影导演，所以只需要每个月，甚至每个季度，做几个重要的战略决策，但这次决策一旦制定，就很难改变。皮克斯的工作节奏比苹果要慢得多，但如果你决定沿着一条路走下去，就不能回头了。

《超越无限》，2007年

We don't think one company can do everything. So you've got to partner with people that are really good at stuff...We're not trying to be great at search, so we partner with people who are great at search... We know how to do the best map clients in the world, but we don't know how to do the back end, so we partner with people that know how to do the back end. And what we want to do is be that consumer's device and that consumer's experience wrapped around all this information and things we can deliver to them in a wonderful user interface, in a coherent product.

D5 Conference: All Things Digital,May30, 2007

I get 50 cents a year for showing up... and the other 50 cents is based on my performance.

AppleInsider. com, May 10, 2007

What's really interesting is if you look at the reason that the iPod exists and that Apple's in that marketplace, it's because these really great Japanese consumer electronics companies who kind of own the portable music market, invented it and owned it, couldn't do the appropriate software, couldn't conceive of and implement the appropriate software. Because an iPod's really just software·It's software in the iPod itself, it's software on the PC or the Mac, and it's software in the cloud for the store.

D5 Conference All Things Digital, May 30, 2007

我们从不认为一个公司可以无所不能。所以你必须寻找一个在擅长于某方面的合作伙伴……我们自己的搜索技术不行，所以我们就要找一个精通此道的合作伙伴……我们知道怎么做成世界上最好的电用户界面子地图客户端，但我们不知道后端技术要如何实现，所以我们就要找一个通晓后端技术的合作伙伴。而我们想做的，是我们提供给消费者一系列的有着精妙用户界面的产品，让消费者的设备选择和用户体验是围绕着我们提供给他们的关于这些产品的资讯来进行。

我每年得到50美分，这是我过来上班的报酬……另外的50美分，是我表现的报酬。

AppleInsider.com，2007年5月10日

如果你能研究一下iPod成功的原因，你会发现真的挺有趣的，这是因为之前独霸音乐市场的日本消费电子公司，没有开发出来合适的软件并广泛应用。因为其实说到底，iPod不过是款软件而已，是PC或者Mac的软件，是商店中云计算的软件。

When we create stuff,we do it because we listen to customers, get their inputs and also throw in what we'd like to see, too. We cook up new products. You never really know if people will love them as much as you do.

CNBC. com, September 5,2007

Every once in a while a revolutionary product comes along that changes everything. One is very fortunate if you get to work on just one of these in your career. Apple's been very fortunate it's been able to introduce a few of these into the world.

Announcement of the iPhone, January 9, 2007

Today, we're introducing three revolutionary products of this class. The first one is a widescreen iPod with touch controls. The second is a revolutionary mobile phone. And the third is a breakthrough Internet communications device. Are you getting it? These are not three separate devices, this is one device, and we are calling it iPhone.

Announcement of the iPhone, January 9, 2007

iPhone is five years ahead of what everybody else has got. If we didn't do one more thing we'd be set for five years!

Newsweek,January 9, 2007

我们之所以发明某个产品，全是我们倾听顾客心声的结果，那里面集中了顾客的要求和我们的判断。每当我们鼓捣出来一个新产品，永远都不会知道人们会不会能像我们自己一样喜欢它。

CNBC.com，2007年9月5日

每隔一段时间，就会有一款革命性的产品横空出世，改变一切。如果你在工作中能够用到一款这样的产品，你就是非常幸运的。苹果已向全球推出几款这样的产品，因此苹果也是非常幸运的。

宣布iPhone智能手机，2007年1月9日

今天，我们将推出三款这一水准的革命性产品。第一个是宽屏触控式iPod，第二个是一款革命性的手机，第三个是突破性的互联网通信设备。你们明白了吗？这不是三台独立的设备，而是一台设备，我们称它为iPhone。

宣布iPhone智能手机，2007年1月9日

iPhone的技术领先了其他手机五年的时间，如果我们不继续做下去，我们就要再准备五年！

《新闻周刊》，2007年1月9日

I have received hundreds of emails from iPhone customers who are upset about Apple dropping the price of iPhone by $200 two months after it went on sale. After reading every one of these mails, I have some observations and conclusions...There is always change and improvement, and there is always someone who bought a product before a particular cutoff date and misses the new price or the new operating system or the new whatever. This is life in the technology lane. If you always wait for the next price cut or to buy the new improved model, you'LL never buy any technology product because there is always something better and less expensive on the horizon...Even though we are making the right decision to lower the price of iPhone, and even though the technology road is bumpy, we need to do a better job of taking care of our early iPhone customers as we aggressively go after new ones with a lower price. Our early customers trusted us, and we must live up to that trust with our actions in moments like these.

Apple Website,September 2007

We do no market research. We don't hire consultants...We just want to make great products.

CNN Money / Fortune, February 2008

The reports of my death are greatly exaggerated.

Apple event for the iPod,September 9, 2008

我收到过好几百封来自iPhone用户的电子邮件，他们都在抱怨iPhone上市两个月之后，价格就下降了200美元，把这些邮件逐一读完之后，我得出了结论…… 变化无时不有，进步无处不在，这难免让人错过某次价格大优惠，或者某次操作系统大换血，或者某次别的什么。这就是科技行业的规律。若是为此缩手缩脚，总是等待新一轮的降价或新款机型，那你永远不会拥有什么电子产品了，因为总是会有更好的更便宜的东西浮现出来……不过就算这次iPhone降价的决定没有错，就算科技行业变化莫测的因素，但在我们用降价来吸引新顾客的同时，也需要更加周到的工作来让老顾客满意。我们的老顾客信任我们，我们也必将不辜负这份信任，在此时用行动来证明一切。

苹果官网，2007年9月

　　我们不做市场调查。我们不请咨询专家……我们只想做出伟大的产品。

美国有线电视新闻网财经频道/《财富》杂志，2008年2月

　　（当彭博社不负责任地草率宣布他已经过世的消息时，他引用了马克·吐温的名言）那些说我已经死了的报道都太离谱。

苹果iPod发布会，2008年9月9日

Mobile devices are really important to people. It's not like this is an obscure product category that affects just a small part of the population. People have seen in the demos and our ads something they instantly know they can figure out how to use. People throw technology at US constantly and most of US say"I don't have time to figure that out. "Most of US have experiences with our current mobile phones and can't figure them out.

USA Today July28,2007

We're in uncharted territory. We've never sold this many of anything before.

Apple keynote address,September 12, 2006

It was one of the first times I started thinking that maybe Thomas Edison did a lot more to improve the world than Karl Marx and Hindu guru Neem Karoli Baba put together.

Steve Jobs: *The Brilliant Mind Behind Apple*, 2009

We have a major opportunity to influence where Apple is going. As every day passes, the work fifty people are doing here is going to send a giant ripple through the universe. I am really impressed with the quality of our ripple. I know I might be a little hard to get on with, but this is the most fun I've had in my life. I'm having a blast.

*Return to the Little Kingdom,*2009

移动设备对于人们来说真的很重要。这和那些只有少数人会关心的难懂的产品目录不一样。人们看过样机和广告之类的东西之后，就能立刻明白如何使用。消费者不断把新技术扔给我们，而我们大部分人会说"我没时间去研究这个"——我们把眼前的手机玩儿得滚瓜烂熟，都不理解是怎么回事儿。

《今日美国》，
2007 年 7 月 28 日

我们处于一片未知的领域，我们之前从来没有卖出去过这么多产品。

苹果主题演讲，
2006 年 9 月 12 日

这是我第一次开始思考，在给世界带来进步方面，也许托马斯·爱迪生的贡献比卡尔·马克思和印度高僧尼姆·卡洛里·巴巴加在一起还要多得多。

《苹果背后的聪明头脑》，
史蒂夫·乔布斯著，2009 年

苹果将要做的事情，会带来巨大的影响，这是我们的一个重要的机会。随着时间一天天过去，五十个人的工作会在宇宙中激荡起巨大的涟漪，我真的为此而感动。我知道我可能很难继续和你们一起奋斗，但这会是我一生中最有趣的事情，我玩得很开心。

《回到小王国》，2009 年

As many of you know,I have been losing weight throughout 2008. The reason   has been a mystery to me and my doctors. A few weeks ago, I decided that getting to the root cause of this and reversing it needed to become my #1 priority. Fortunately,after further testing, my doctors think they have found the cause—a hormone imbalance that has been robbing me of the proteins my body needs to be healthy Sophisticated blood tests have confirmed this diagnosis…So now I've said more than I wanted to say,and all that I am going to say,about this.

Apple Website. January 5, 2009

In order to take myself out of the lime light and foCUS on my health, and to allow everyone at Apple to focus on delivering extraordinary products, I have decided to take a medical leave of absence until the end of June.

Apple media advisory to all Apple employees, January14, 2009

I have asked Tim Cook to be responsible for Apple's day to day operations, and I know he and the rest of the executive management team will do a great job. As CEO, I plan to remain involved in major strategic decisions while I am out. Our board of directors fully supports this plan.

正如你们很多人知道的，自2008年以来，我的体重一直在下降。我和我的医生都未能搞清楚原因所在。几周前，我决定彻查其根本原因，并将此列为我的首要任务。幸运的是，在接受了进一步检查之后，我的医生们认为，他们找到了原因——荷尔蒙失衡。正是这一原因导致我体内蛋白质减少。深入的血检也证明了这一点。……这就是这段时间以来我一直想说的话，关于我的健康问题。

苹果官网，2009年1月5日

一方面是为了把自己从公众的关注中解脱出来，专注在自身健康上；另一方面也是为了让苹果员工都能专心于创造非凡的产品，因此我决定休病假，直到六月底。

我让蒂姆·库克负责苹果公司的日常运作，我相信他和其他的高管团队能做得很好。作为CEO，在休假期间我还是会参与重要的战略决策的制定，董事会对我的计划也非常支持。

对苹果全部员工发布的媒体报告，2009年1月14日

Originally,we weren't exactly sure how to market the Touch. Was it an iPhone without the phone? Was it a pocket computer? What happened was, what customers told us was, they started to see it as a game machine. We started to market it that way,and it just took off. And now what we really see is it's the lowest-cost way to the App Store, and that's the big draw. So what we were focused on is just reducing the price to$199. We don't need to add new stuff,We need to get the price down where everyone can afford it.

New York Times, September 9, 2009

Even though we've been using these internally for some time and working on it for a few years, you still have butterflies in your stomach the week before…the night before introduction…the launch…You never know until you get it into your customers'hands and they tell you what they think. The feedback we've got has been off the charts. We think this is a profound game-changer. We think when people look back some number of years from now, they'll see this as a major event in personal computation devices. What's been really great for me is how quickly people have got it. You know ,I've gotten a few thousand E-mails from people I've never talked to before just telling me how much they think this product is going to change their life and what they do. People are getting it very quickly.

Apple event for iPhone 4.0 software, April 8,2010

起初，我们不是很确定应该如何去做Touch的市场推广工作。这是个不能打电话的iPhone？是个可以装进兜里的电脑？事实是，顾客告诉我们他们最开始把这当成了一部游戏机，于是我们也用这个特点来进行市场营销，获得了市场的肯定。而实际上，我们现在已经把Touch看成了使用App Store的最低成本的方式，这是个很具有吸引力的卖点。所以我们现在要做的是把Touch的价格降到199美元，让每个人都能够承受得起，而不是增加一些别的什么东西。

《纽约时报》，
2009年9月9日

就算我们内部已经试用了一阵子，就算为了开发它已经花费数年的心血，在正式发布的前夜，你仍然会觉得忐忑不安，如果不把它交到顾客的手里，如果不能听到他们的想法，你永远不知道这东西究竟怎么样。结果，我们收到的用户反馈超乎想象得好。这是一款有着深远意义的游戏变革产品，我们觉得如果若干年后再回头看，iPad的出现会成为个人电脑设备发展历程中的一个重大事件。而对我来说，更重要的是，人们购买iPad的速度居然如此之快。我收到了几千封电子邮件 —— 都是一些素不相识的陌生人，他们告诉我这个产品给他们的生活带来了多么大的变化，人们购买iPad的速度真是太快了。

iPhone 4.0软件发布会，
2010年4月8日

I'm sure there will always be dedicated devices, and they may have a few   advantages in doing just one thing. But I think the general—purpose devices will win the day. Because I think people just probably aren't willing to pay for a dedicated device.

New York Times, September 9, 2009

So far I have to say, that people seem to be liking the iPad. You know I mean we've sold one every three seconds since we launched it… Right now I'm just worried that it's taking us three whole seconds to make one.

interview at D8 in 2010

Netbooks aren't better than anything. They're just cheap laptops.

Apple event for iPad1,January27,2010

Sure, what we do has to make commercial sense, but it's never the starting point. We start with the product and the user experience.

Time, April 1, 2010

You're headed for a one-term presidency.

Steve Jobs, Jobs said to Obama in 2010

A lot of companies have chosen to downsize, and maybe that was the right thing for them. We chose a different path. Our belief was that if we kept putting great products in front of customers, they would continue to open their wallets.

Success, June 2010

我相信总会有一些专用的设备,他们专注于某一项功能,可能会有优势。但我想真正能占上风的还是通用型的设备,因为我觉得人们可能不会愿意去花钱买一个只能干一件事的机器。

《纽约时报》,
2009年9月9日

　　我现在不得不说,人们似乎很喜欢iPad产品。我的意思是,从发布这个产品开始,我们每三秒就能卖出一台……现在我担心的是,我们生产一台需要整整三秒的时间。

D8峰会上的访谈,2010年

　　上网本除了便宜,没什么可取之处。

苹果的iPad1发布会,
2010年1月27日

　　当然,我们的所作所为包含着商业因素,但商业因素从来不是我们的出发点,我们的出发点是产品以及用户体验。

《时代》杂志,
2010年4月1日

　　看样子,你就想当一届总统吧。

《史蒂夫·乔布斯传》,
2010年乔布斯对奥巴马说

　　很多公司都选择了裁员,这对他们来说或许是个明智之选。但我们选择了一条不同的道路。我们相信如果能够一直把卓越的产品呈现给消费者,他们就会继续掏出钱包。

《成功》杂志,
2010年6月

Apple's grown like a weed, and as you know, we've always been in the corner of the ends in 280. and those buildings hold maybe 2600 people or 2800 people. But we've got almost 12000people in the area. So we're renting buildings-not very good buildings either, at an ever-greater radius from our campus and we're putting people in those. And it is clear that we need to build a new campus, so we just add space. That doesn't mean we don't need the one we got, we need it, but we need another one to augment it. So we've got a plan that let's stay in Cupertino.

Steve Jobs' last public speech in the meeting of Cupertino City in 2011

We're the largest tax payer in Cupertino, so we'd like to continue to stay here and pay taxes. That's number one… And number two, we employ some really talented great people and across the whole age spectrum. A lot of people right out of college, hire a lot of Stanford grads, etc, and you know people that are in their 50s and even 60s, like me, I'm in my 50s.

Steve Jobs' last public speech in the meeting of Cupertino City in 2011

Innovation distinguishes between a leader and a follower.

The Innovation Secrets of Steve Jobs, 2011

苹果如雨后春笋般快速发展着，而库比蒂诺一直是我们钟爱的地方。从开始的办公室到现在的280号公路尽头的拐弯处的办公大楼。这几栋楼能容纳2600到2800名员下，可实际上我们这个区的员工数量超过了12000。不得已只能租些离国区很远的差劲的写字楼给员工办公。很显然我们需要修建新的园区，所以增加了地方。但是这不表示我们就不需要现在的办公楼，我们只是需要增加点新的地方。我们计划就待在库比蒂诺了。

乔布斯在库比蒂诺市议会最后的公开演讲，2011年

我们是库比蒂诺的纳税大户，我们很高兴能留下来继续缴税，这是第一点……此外，我们雇佣了很多优秀人才，各个年龄阶段的人都有，很多是刚毕业的大学生，比如斯坦福大学等，还有50、60岁的员工，像我就是。

乔布斯在库比蒂诺市议会最后的公开演讲，2011年

领袖和跟风者的区别就在于创新。

《史蒂夫·乔布斯的创新秘密》，2011

I've said this before, but thought it was worth repeating: It's in Apple's DNA that technology alone is not enough. That it's technology married with liberalarts, married with the humanities, that yields us the result that makes our hearts sing. And nowhere is that more true than in these post-PC devices.

And a lot of folks in this tablet market are rushing in and they're looking at this as the next PC. The hardware and the software are done by different companies. And they're talking about speeds and feeds just like they did with PCs. And our experience and every bone in our body says that that is not the right approach to this. That these are post-PC devices that need to be even easier to use than a PC. That need to be even more intuitive than a PC. And where the SOftware and the hardware and the applications need to intertwine in an even more seamless way than they do on a PC.

And we think we're on the right track with this. We think we have the right architecture not just insilicon, but in the organization to build these kinds of products.

And so I think we stand a pretty good chance of being pretty competitive in this market. And I hope that what you've seen today gives you a good feel for that.

Apple event for iPad 2, March 2, 2011

下面这些话我之前说过，但还是有必要再重复一次：苹果的DNA就是，仅有技术是不够的。只有技术与综合学科联姻，与人文科学联姻，才能产生让我们心灵为之共鸣的效果，这些后PC时代的电子设备就是最为有力的证明。

现在有许多人抢着进入平板电脑市场，他们认为这就是下一代的个人电脑。这些产品的软硬件由许多不同的公司开发。他们也像讨论个人电脑一样，在讨论平板电脑的速度和信号。而在我们看来，我们深知这并不是开发平板电脑的正确途径。这些后个人电脑设备应该比个人电脑更好上手，更加简单与直观，而且他们的软件，硬件以及应用应该更好地融合在一起。而且，我们认为我们走在正确的道路上。我们相信我们所拥有的正确的架构不仅仅是关乎产品本身，更多的是我们拥有一个能开发这种产品的正确的组织氛围。

所以，我觉得我们正处在市场竞争中一个不错的优势位置。而且我希望你们今天看到的这些能让你们深切地体会到这一点。

苹果的iPad2发布会，2011年3月2日

One of the things I learned at Pixar is the technology industries and the content industries do not understand each other. In Silicon Valley and at most technology companies, I swear that most people think the creative process is a bunch of guys in their early 30s, sitting on a couch, drinking beer and thinking of jokes. No, they really do. That's how television is made, they think; that is how movies are made. People in Hollywood and in the content industries, they think technology is something you just write a check for and buy. They don't understand the creativity element of technology. These are like ships passing in the night.

*CNNTech,*June10,2011

我在皮克斯公司学到了一件事，那就是，科技产业和内容产业之间对彼此都知之甚少。我敢肯定，无论是在硅谷还是大多数的技术公司里面的大部分人，都会认为所谓创意过程，就是一群三十岁出头的家伙，窝在沙发里，喝着啤酒想笑话。而他们真正的工作，其实是思考如何制造电视机，思考如何拍摄电影；而好莱坞和内容产业的人呢，他们也会认为科技产业不过就是一帮人写写支票，买买东西，谁都没明白科技里面蕴含的创造性元素。这事儿就像一条在夜里摸黑航行的船。

美国有线电视新闻网技术频道，2011 年 6 月 10 日

8. 谢幕

Farewell

2011年3月16日，美国加州，苹果CEO史蒂夫·乔布斯外出，越发消瘦的他身体状况令人堪忧，但这并未影响他对苹果、对公司的热忱。

Apple CEO Steve Jobs appears to have lost more weight since he was last,but it seems that his enthusiasm on Apple is not affected.

2004年8月1日
乔布斯首次透露其患有癌症消息

2006年6月1日
乔布斯表示他被诊断患有胰腺癌

2008年7月23日
乔布斯表示，他身上已没有毒瘤

2008年12月16日
苹果表示乔布斯将缺席Macworld

2009年1月5日
乔布斯称患有荷尔蒙失调症

2009年1月14日
乔布斯病休，COO库克暂时接替

2009年6月23日
医院证实乔布斯进行了肝脏移植

2009年6月29日
苹果宣布乔布斯重返公司

2009年9月9日
乔布斯病休后首次出席发布会

2011年1月17日
乔布斯因健康原因将再次休假

2011年10月6日
乔布斯去世

Steve Jobs
史蒂夫·乔布斯
1955-2011

乔布斯健康状况回顾 | Steve Jobs Health Status
Review

10月5日，"果粉"和员工
献花悼念乔布斯

Apple Fans and staffs lay
flowers to mourn Jobs,
October 5

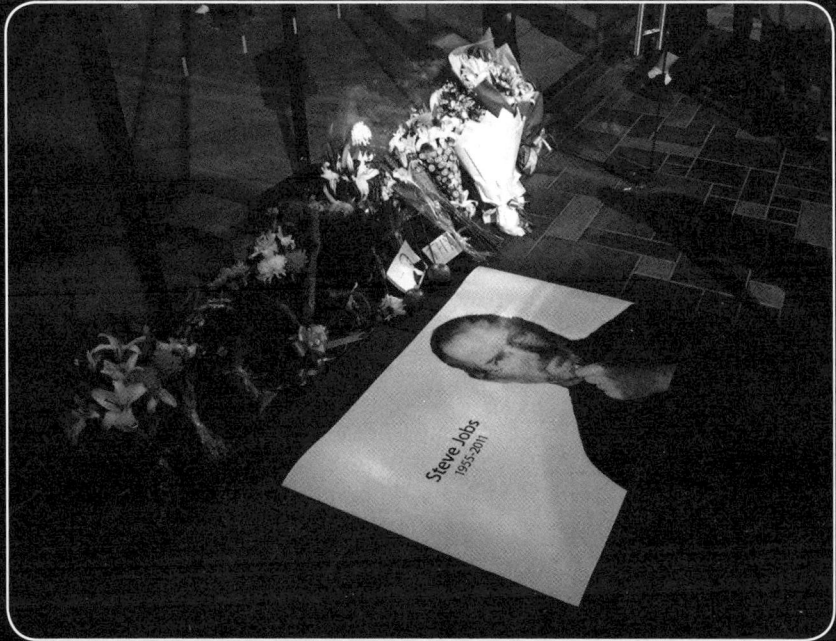

永别了，乔布斯！　　　　Farewell, Steve Jobs

I mean, some people say, "Oh, God, if Jobs got run over by a bus, Apple would be in trouble." And, you know, I think it wouldn't be a party, but there are really capable people at Apple. My job is to make the whole executive team good enough to be successors, so that's what I try to do.

CNN Money

I hereby resign as CEO of Apple. I would like to serve, if the Board sees fit, as Chairman of the Board, director and Apple employee. As far as my successor goes, I strongly recommend that we execute our succession plan and name Tim Cook as CEO of Apple. I believe Apple's brightest and most innovative days are ahead of it. And I look forward to watching and contributing to its success in a new role.

Resignation letter, August 2011

We're born, we live for a brief instant, and we die. It's been happening for a long time. Technology is not changing it much—if at all.

Wired, February 1996

We don't get a chance to do that many things, and every one should be really excellent, because this is our life. Life is brief, and then you die, you know? And we've all chosen to do this with our lives. So it better be damn good. It better be worth it.

Fortune

我想说的是，有些人会说："天啊！如果史蒂夫出了车祸，苹果就要完蛋了。"可是你要知道，这虽然不是什么好事，但对于 CEO 的问题，董事会有一些不错的备选人。我的工作就是锻炼高层管理团队，让他们有成为接班人的资格，这就是我所努力的工作。

美国有线电视新闻网财经频道

我宣布辞去苹果CEO的职位，如果董事会同意，我将担任苹果董事会主席。对于接任者，我强烈建议执行我们制定的接任计划，提名蒂姆·库克为苹果CEO。我相信，苹果的未来将更加光明，更具创造力。同时，我期待未来苹果的成功，也期待能为此尽自己的绵薄之力。

辞职信，2011 年 8 月

我们呱呱坠地来到人间，经历短暂的一生，然后无可避免地衰老死去。这是千古不变的规律。

《连线》杂志，1996 年 2 月

人这辈子没法做太多事情，所以每一件都要做到精彩绝伦。因为，这就是我们的宿命。人生苦短，你明白吗？而这就是我们为人生做出的选择。所以这件事情最好能够做好一点，最好能够物有所值。

《财富》杂志

We're here to put a dent in the universe. Otherwise why else even be here?

MacWorld

ne wants to die, even people who want to go to Heaven don't want to die to get there, and yet, death is the destination we all share. No one has ever escaped it. And that is as it should be.

Stanford Commencement Speech, June2005

That's why I think death is the most wonderful invention of life. It purges the system of these old models that are obsolete. I think that's one of Apple's challenges, really. When two young people walk in with the next thing, are we going to embrace it and say this is fantastic? Are you going to be willing to drop our models, or are we going to explain it away?I think we'll do better , because we're completely aware of it and we make it a priority.

Playboy, February 1985

Death is very likely the single best invention of life. It's life's change agent; it clears out the old to make way for the new. Right now, the new is you. But someday, not too long from now, you will gradually become the old and be cleared away. Sorry to be so dramatic, but it's quite true.

Stanford Commencement Speech, June2005

活着就是为了改变世界，难道还有其他原因吗？

MacWorld

没有人愿意死，即使那些想上天堂的人们，也想活着上天堂。但是死亡是我们共同的归宿，没有人能逃得过它，这是上天注定的。

斯坦福毕业典礼演讲，2005 年 6 月

这就是为什么我认为死亡是生命最奇妙的发明。它净化了陈旧的、过时的模式系统。我觉得这个对苹果来说，是一次艰巨的任务。当两个年轻人偷偷进行了下一件事情，我们会张开双臂欢迎，称赞真是不可思议吗？我们会想要摒弃现有的模式吗？或者我们会为他们辩解，消除他们的紧张吗？我认为我们可以做得比这些更好，因为我们已经完全意识到了这一点，并提高了它的优先级。

《花花公子》杂志，1985 年 2 月

死亡简直就是生命中最棒的发明，是生命变化的媒介，送走老人们，给新生代留下空间。现在你们是新生代，但是不久的将来，你们也会逐渐变老，被送出人生的舞台。很抱歉讲得这么戏剧化，但是这是真的。

斯坦福毕业典礼演讲，2005 年 6 月

Your time is limited, so don't waste it living someone else's life. Don't be trapped by dogma - which is living with the results of other people's thinking. Don't let the noise of other's opinions drown out your own inner voice. And most important, have the courage to follow your heart and intuition. They somehow already know what you truly want to become. Everything else is secondary.

Stanford Commencement Speech, June2005

We are deeply saddened to announce that Steve Jobs passed away today.

Steve's brilliance, passion and energy were the source of countless innovations that enrich and improve all of our lives. The world is immeasurably better because of Steve.

His greatest love was for his wife, Laurene, and his family. Our hearts go out to them and to all who were touched by his extraordinary gifts.

Statement by Apple's Board of Directors, October 5, 2011

你们的时间很有限，所以不要将他们浪费在重复其他人的生活上。不要被教条束缚，那意味着你和其他人思考的结果一起生活。不要被其他人喧嚣的观点掩盖你真正的内心的声音。还有最重要的是，你要有勇气去听从你直觉和心灵的指示 —— 它们在某种程度上知道你想要成为什么样子，所有其他的事情都是次要的。

斯坦福毕业典礼演讲，2005 年 6 月

　　我们（苹果董事会）今天沉痛宣告史蒂夫·乔布斯逝世。

苹果董事会致乔布斯逝世悼词，2011 年 10 月 5 日

　　乔布斯才华出众，充满激情与活力，他是数不清的创新之源，这些创新丰富和改善了人们的生活。因为史蒂夫，世界变得更加美好的程度是不可估量的。

　　他伟大的爱留给了他的妻子劳伦和他的家庭，谨向他们，向所有被他超凡天赋触动的人们聊表心意。

Um, Guys, STILL HERE!

附录：乔布斯大事年表

Milestones

Milestones

SJ born in San Francisco to Abdulfattah John Jandali and Joanne Simpson. He is given up for adoption to Paul and Clara Jobs, who name him Steven Paul Jobs. (February 24)	**1955**
The Jobs family moves to Los Altos, California, and Sj enters Homestead High School, where he develops an interest in music(especially Bob Dylan and the Beatles)and electronics.	**1966**
SJ meets future Apple cofounder Stephen "Woz" Wozniak.	**1971**
sJ and Wozniak build and sell illegal tone generators called"blue boxes"to college students who use them to make free phone calls. (An October 1971 article in Esquire explained how to make them.)They illicitly earn$6, 000 before moving on to legitimate ventures. SJ graduates from high school . He enrolls in Reed College(Portland, Oregon)in September, but drops out after one semester, though he continues to audit classes while living a bohemian lifestyle. At Reed, SJ meets future Apple employee Dan Kottke, who would later go on to assemble and test the first Apple I computer.	**1972**

乔布斯大事年表

1955

乔布斯出生在三藩市，亲生父母是阿卜杜法塔赫·约翰·钱德里和乔安妮·辛普森，出生之后，被亲生父母遗弃，由保罗·乔布斯(Paul Jobs)和克拉拉·乔布斯(Clara Jobs)夫妇收养，取名史蒂夫·保罗·乔布斯。(2月24日)

1966

乔布斯一家搬到了加利福尼亚州洛斯拉图斯，乔布斯进入家园高中，这里培养了他对音乐(特别市对鲍勃·迪伦和披头士)和电子学的兴趣。

1971

遇到了未来苹果公司的合伙创始人 —— 史蒂芬·沃兹尼亚克。

1972

史蒂夫和沃兹一起做出了一部非法的音频发声器，起名为"蓝盒子"，这可以让大学生们免费盗打电话(1971年10月号的《老爷》杂志中有一篇文章讲述了他们制作这个东西的过程)，靠着蓝盒子，他们挣到了6000美金的非法收入。

史蒂夫高中毕业后，同年9月份进入里德学院(学校位于俄勒冈州的波特兰)继续大学课程，但在一个学期后退学，之后，他一边过着自由自在的日子，一边自学审计学课程。

SJ takes a job at Nolan Bushnell's video game company, twAtari. (September)

SJ begins attending the Homebrew Computer Club, composed of electronics hobbyists.

Apple Computer moves to Stevens Creek Boulevard in Cupertino, California, its first office building. (January)

Apple is cofounded by SJ(45%share), Wozniak (45%share), and Ronald Wayne (10 %share). Wayne decides he can't take the risk and sells his 10%share of Apple back to SJ and Wozfor$800. (April1)

SJ gets an order for 50 computers from the Byte Shop in Mountain View, California. The owner is expecting turnkey computers, but Apple delivers only the heart of the computer, the circuit board. SJ expected computer hobbyists to add the requisite peripherals themselves: a keyboard, a monitor(a CRT television set), a power supply, and a case. (July)

SJ and Kottke exhibit the Apple I at the Personal Computer Festival in Atlantic City, New Jersey. Meanwhile, Wozniak works on Apple II, a major leap forward-a mass market, ready-to-use-out-of-the-box personal computer. (August 28-29)

In exchange for a one—third interest in Apple, Mike Markkula, a venture capitalist, "supplie[s]$250, 000 initial financial backing"(Apple Computer Inc. , Offering Memorandum). (January)

乔布斯进入诺兰·布什内尔创办的视频游戏公司雅达利工作。（9月）

乔布斯加入了由电子爱好者组成的"家酿计算机俱乐部"。

苹果电脑公司搬到了加利福尼亚州库比蒂诺市的史蒂文斯溪大道 —— 他们第一个办公楼的所在地。（1月）

史蒂夫、沃兹、和罗纳德·韦尼在苹果公司所占股份分别为45%、45%和10%，后来韦尼感到风险太大，把10%的股份以800美金的价格卖给了史蒂夫和沃兹。（4月1日）

史蒂夫拿到了一张50台电脑的订单，这张订单来自加州山景城的一家电脑商店，店主希望可以买到能装配完整的电脑，但苹果当时只能提供电路板。于是乔布斯希望依靠电脑发烧友们自己把所需要的外设加上：键盘、显示器（CRT），电源以及机箱。（7月）

乔布斯和科特肯带着Apple I参加了纽泽西的大西洋城参加个人电脑节的展览，与此同时，沃兹正在研发Apple II —— 一个巨大的飞跃，而大众市场，已经准备好了迎接"走出盒子"的个人电脑时代的到来。（8月28-29日）

风险投资人麦克·马库拉注资25万美金作为初始资金，获得了苹果三分之一的股份。（1月）

Apple debuts the Apple II at the West Coast Computer Faire in San Francisco. (April 16—17)

Apple ships its first Apple II system. (June)

Apple shows its first floppy disk drive for the Apple II at the Consumer Electronics Show(CES)in Las Vegas. (January)

1978

Apple ships the Apple III for the business market in the fall, as SJ focuses on creating the first Lisa computer for the business market. Apple recruits Michael Scott from National Semiconductor to serve as its CEO. (February)

SJ has his first child, Lisa Brennan-Jobs, with then-girlfriend Chris Ann Brennan. He assumes no role in raising her, and refuses to accept paternity until a court ordered test proves high probability for a DNA match.

Apple earns$47 million in revenues. SJ and other key staffers from Apple visit Xerox PARC(Palo Alto Research Center), where they are exposed to new computer technologies, including the mouse and the graphical user interface(GUI). It is a fortuitous event for SJ, who immediately grasps their implications for the future of computers. Apple debuts Apple Plus. (June)

1979

VisiCalc, an electronic spread sheet program, is released for the Apple II, which helps spur sales of the computer. (November)

苹果在西岸计算机展发布了Apple II。
（4月16-17日）

苹果推出了第一版Apple II系统。（6月）

在拉斯维加斯的国际消费电子展上，苹果展示了他们的为Apple II设计的第一款软磁盘驱动。（1月）

就在乔布斯专注于开发第一代Apple Lisa的时候，苹果在当年秋天推出了第一款商用计算机 —— Apple III。迈克尔·斯考特从美国国家半导体公司来到苹果，担任苹果首任CEO。（2月）

乔布斯和女友克莉丝·安·布伦南生下了他的第一个孩子 —— 丽莎·布伦南·乔布斯。但他没有承担起养育孩子的责任，之后也拒绝承认是孩子的父亲，直到法庭命令他们去做DNA测试后，配型成功才承认。

苹果收入激增到四千七百万美元，乔布斯和苹果公司的一些高层人员拜访了帕罗奥图研究中心，他们在那里看到了包括鼠标和图形用户界面在内的新的计算机技术。这次拜访给乔布斯带来了好运，他马上就看到了这些技术对未来计算机的影响，同年，苹果公司推出了Apple Plus。（6月）

电子数据表程序程序 —— VisiCalc，被应用于Apple II，大大刺激了Apple II的销量。（11月）

The Apple IPO sells 4. 6 million shares. Initially priced at $22 per share, the stock closes at$29. Apple's valuation: $1, 778 billion. (December 12)

Apple debuts the Apple III; its design flaws result in a recall of its first 14, 000 units. Programmer Andy Hertzfeld of Apple begins work on the operating system for the Macintosh, an affordable alternative to SJ's expensive Lisa computer. (February)

On a day dubbed"Black Wednesday"by Apple employees, Apple's CEO Mike Scott, without seeking management approval from the board of directors, fires half of the Apple II team. In turn, the board fires Scott, appoints Markkula as interim CEO, and begins a search for a new CEO. (February 25)

SJ becomes chairman of the board. Markkula becomes president, replacing Scott. (March)

IBM introduces its personal computer, the IBM PC 5150, which SJ publicly derides as technologically inferior; SJ underestimates its appeal, especially to the business community, which prefers it to Apple's products. (August)

Microsoft signs a deal to develop three much-needed applications for the Mac: a spreadsheet, a database, and a business graphics program. (January 22)

苹果公司上市，每股初始价22美元，共发行了460万股，发行当天收盘价29美元，公司总价值1万7千7百8十亿美元。（12月12日）

1980

Apple III上市销售；因为设计缺陷，导致14000台机器被召回。苹果程序员安迪·赫茨菲尔德开始开发Mac机——一款比Lisa更有价格优势的替代的操作系统。（2月）

1981

苹果员工称为"黑色星期三"，苹果CEO麦克·斯考特，在没有得到董事会批准的情况下，一口气解雇了Apple II团队的一半员工，于是，董事会也解雇了斯考特，由马库拉暂代CEO一职，同时开始物色新CEO的人选。（2月25日）

乔布斯出任公司董事会主席，马库拉代替斯考特担任公司总经理。（3月）

IBM发布了个人电脑——IBM PC 5150，乔布斯用"粗制滥造"来形容它。但乔布斯低估了IBM PC 5150的市场吸引力，特别是对一些商业用户来说，比起苹果的产品，他们更中意IBM。（8月）

微软和苹果签订开发协议，为Mac开发三款重要的应用软件：表格程序、数据库以及商业绘图软件。（1月22日）

1982

SJ appears on Time magazine for its cover story, "America's Risk Takers: Steven Jobs of Apple Computer." (February 15)

SJ buys an apartment in New York City in the San Remo building. After extensive renovations by architect I. M. Pei, SJ never moves in, and later sells it.

Time overlooks SJ for "Man of the Year" in favor of his creation, dubbing the personal computer as "machine of the year. "(December)

1983

SJ goes to New York City to give the media a first look at its powerful business computer, Lisa. While there, he meets, and is favorably impressed with, PepsiCo executive John Scully, whom he eventually woos to Apple. (January)

Apple officially releases the Lisa (Local Integrated Software Architecture) computer. (January 19)

Apple debuts the Apple IIe. (January)

Apple hires Sculley as its CEO. (April 8)

1984

Apple debuts the first Macintosh computer, launching with a groundbreaking TV commercial airing during Super Bowl XVIII. Called "1984, "and directed by Ridley Scott, it cost $1.2 million to produce and air. The "Mac" is the world's first mass—market GUI(graphical user interface)computer. (January 22)

乔布斯成为当月《时代》杂志的封面人物，并配有封面故事"美国冒险家 —— 苹果电脑的史蒂夫·乔布斯"。（2月15日）

乔布斯在纽约买下了一套SanRemo公寓楼，并请建筑师贝聿铭进行了大刀阔斧的改造，但他从未入住过，之后就把这栋房子出售了。

鉴于乔布斯的创新，《时代》杂志把乔布斯评为"年度人物"，将个人电脑评为"年度机器"。（12月）

1983

乔布斯前往纽约，把第一款旗舰商用计算机Lisa呈现在了媒体面前。就在那时，百事可乐的执行官约翰·斯卡利给乔布斯留下了深刻印象，最终被乔布斯挖到了苹果。（1月）

苹果正式发布Lisa（局部集成软件架构）电脑。（1月19日）

苹果推出Apple IIe。（1月）

苹果任命斯卡利为CEO。（4月8日）

1984

苹果推出第一款Mac机，在美国国家橄榄球联盟超级碗第18届橄榄球赛节目转播中，播放了雷德利·斯科特导演的60秒Mac电视广告"1984"，广告的制作和播出费用达一百二十万美元。Mac是世界上第一台使用图形用户界面（GUI）的电脑。（1月22日）

Lisa 2 debuts. (January 14)

SJ purchases Jackling House, a 17,250-square-foot mansion in Woodside, California.

Apple buys all 39 pages of available advertising space in Newsweek'S "Election Extra"issue in order to promote the Macintosh. (November—December)

The LaserWriter printer announced, speeding the explosion in desktop publishing. Also, Lisa is repositioned as the Macintosh XL, but its sales do not improve. (January)

Wozniak, unhappy with his largely symbolic role at Apple, resigns to found his own company,called CL9, where he can concentrate on his first love: inventing electronic products. (February 6)

Sculley, with the approval of the Apple board of directors, relieves SJ as the head of the Mac division. (In a 2010 interview with Leander Kahney,Sculley graciously acknowledged his mistake in not retaining Jobs: "It's so obvious looking back now that that would have been the right thing to do. We didn't do it, so I blame myself for that one. It would have saved Apple this near-death experience they had. ")(May 31)

Feeling betrayed, and lacking confidence in the future of Apple, SJ keeps one share of Apple stock and sells the rest.

推出 Lisa 2。（1月14日）

乔布斯买下了位于加州半岛伍德赛德镇的一所名叫"Jackling House"的房子，房子总面积17250平方公尺。

为了宣传Mac机，苹果买下了《新闻周刊》总统竞选特刊中39页的广告位。（11-12月）

1985

LaserWriter打印机宣布，他们正在加快桌面排版系统的开发工作。同时，Lisa的升级版Macintosh XL推出，但销量并未因此而增长。（1月）

沃兹因不满在苹果公司有名无实的地位而辞职，创立了自己的CL9公司，专注于电子产品的发明——这也是他最初的兴趣所在。（2月6日）

在苹果董事会的支持下，斯库利免去了乔布斯的Mac部门经理的职务。（2010年，利安得·卡尼采访斯库利时，他坦率了承认了那时辞去乔布斯的做法是错误的："现在回头再看，很明显当时我们本应该有正确的选择，但是我们没那么做，我常常为此自责，如果乔布斯没有离开，苹果不会经历那次危机。"）（5月31日）

乔布斯感到众叛亲离，对苹果公司的未来失去了信心，于是把手中苹果的股票全部卖出，只留下了一股。

Xerox PARC's Alan Kay, a noted computer visionary, tells SJ that George Lucas is looking to sell Pixar.SJ is interested at$10 million, but not at the$30 million asking price. Apple lays off 1, 200 employees.

(June 14)

Macintosh XL is discontinued. (August 10)

sJ goes to Apple's board to announce he's leaving to start a new computer company,NeXT. Apple encourages him, and even offers to be an investment partner. (September 13)

SJ and Wozniak are awarded the National Medal of Technology by President Ronald Reagan.

President and Chief Executive Sculley adds chairman of the board to his duties. (January 29)

1986

Apple retires the original Macintosh and replaces it with the Macintosh 512K Enhanced. (April 14)

SJ buys The Graphics Group(later named Pixar Animation Studios)from George Lucas and invests$10 million. SJ becomes its CEO and majority shareholder. Pixar debuts its graphics workstation, the Pixar Image Computer. (May)

Apple releases the Macintosh SE, and its first color graphics computer, Macintosh II. (March 2)

1987

施乐帕洛阿尔托研究中心的艾伦·凯，对计算机领域有着出色的预见性，他告诉乔布斯说，乔治·卢卡斯正准备卖掉皮克斯。于是，经过一番讨价还价，乔布斯把价格从3千万美金压到了1千万，买下了皮克斯。与此同时，苹果公司裁员1200名。(6月14日)

Macintosh XL停产。(8月10日)

乔布斯向苹果董事会宣布，他准备离开苹果创办NeXT公司。苹果百般挽留，甚至打算让他成为投资伙伴。(9月13日)

乔布斯和沃兹被美国总统罗纳德·里根授予"美国国家技术奖"。

1986

总裁兼行政总裁斯库利成为苹果董事会主席。(1月29日)

原始的Mac机停产，取代它的是Macintosh 512K Enhanced。(4月14日)

乔布斯从乔治·卢卡斯手中买下皮克斯动画工作室，并注资1千万美金，成为皮克斯动画工作室的CEO及主要股东，发布了自己的图形工作站 —— 皮克斯图像电脑。(5月)

1987

苹果发布Macintosh SE和它的第一台彩色图形计算机 —— Macintosh II。(3月2日)

Pixar Image Computer(p-11)ships.

The NeXT computer debuts.(October 12)

1988

Pixar's animated film Tin Toy wins an Academy Award
for Best Animated Short Film.

1989

Apple debuts the Macintosh Portable, which weighs
17 pounds. (September 20)

SJ discontinues development and sales on the Pixar
Image Computer and concentrates on developing its
software called RenderMan. (April 30)

1990

SJ marries Laurene Powell at the Ahwanhee Hotel in
Yosemite National Park. The ceremony is officiated by a Zen
Buddhist monk, Kobin Chino, a friend of SJ's. (March 18)

1991

Pixar and Walt Disney Studios team up to develop,
produce and distribute up to three feature-length
animated films" according to Pixar's website.

Fortune magazine adds SJ to its National Business Hall
of Fame. (April 9)

1992

SJ's biological sister, Mona Simpson, publishes a novel
titled the Lost father.

At CES in Chicago, Sculley shows a prototype of the
Newton Message Pad, Apple's personal digital assistant.
(May)

皮克斯图像电脑正式推出。

NeXT发布。（10月12日） **1988**

皮克斯制作的动画电影《锡铁小兵》获得奥斯卡最佳 **1989**
动画短片奖。

苹果发布Macintosh Portable，重17磅。（9月20日）

乔布斯继续进行皮克斯图像电脑的研发和销售，专 **1990**
注于一款叫做RenderMan的软件开发。（4月30日）

史蒂夫.乔布斯与劳伦.鲍威尔（Laurene Powell） **1991**
在美国优胜美的国家公园的Ahwahnee酒店举行了婚
礼，婚礼仪式由乔布斯的一位朋友，禅宗僧人乙川弘文
主持。（3月18日）

皮克斯和沃尔特·迪斯尼工作共同合作，制作了三部
长篇动画电影。—— 皮克斯官网。

乔布斯跻身《财富杂志》全美商业名人堂。（4月9日） **1992**

乔布斯的胞妹，莫娜·辛普森，发表小说《失去的
父亲》。

在芝加哥国际消费电子展上，斯库利展示了"牛顿
留言板"样机，这是苹果推出的一款个人数字助理设备。
（5月）

Failing to meet sales expectations. NeXT drops its hardware line to focus exclusively on software development. (February 11)

1993

Sculley is replaced as Apple CEO by Michael Spindler·(June 18)

Apple announces major layoffs in the works: 2,500 people worldwide. (July)

Newton ships. (August)

Apple discontinues its Apple II computer and peripherals. (October 15)

Apple debuts its first PowerPC product, a logic board for its Centris and Quadra lines of Mac computers·(January)

1994

Apple announces it will license its OS(System 7)to other computer manufacturers. Its first customers include Radius and Power Computing.

SJ unsuccessfully tries to sell Pixar. Among the suitors: Microsoft.

Pocahontas is previewed in New York City's Central Park(June 10).

1995

Disney releases Toy Story on Thanksgiving weekend. The film is a hit and goes on to gross$191. 7 million in U·S domestic receipts. (November)

因为与消费者期望相去甚远，NeXT放弃了硬件产品线，专注于软件开发。（2月11）

1993

迈克尔·斯平德勒取代斯库利，成为苹果新任CEO。（6月18日）

苹果宣布在世界范围内裁员2500人。（7月）

"牛顿"推出。（8月）

苹果继续开发Apple II及其周边设备。（10月15日）

苹果发布首款PowerPC产品，并把它作为Mac电脑Centris和Quadra产品线的芯片。（1月）

1994

苹果宣布将为其他公司颁布OS（System 7）系统许可证，它的第一批顾客包括Radius 和Power Computing。

乔布斯拒绝了微软抛出的橄榄枝，决定不出手皮克斯公司。

电影《风中奇缘》在纽约中央公园举行试映会。（6月10日）

1995

迪斯尼在感恩节周末推出《玩具总动员》，大获成功，仅在美国国内票房收入就达到了19亿1千7百万美元。（11月）

Pixar's IPO sells 6. 9 million shares. (November 29)

Spindler is replaced as Apple CEO by Gilbert Amelio. Soon after Amelio also assumes the position of chairman. (February 2)

1996

sJ is prominently featured in a PBS documentary about Silicon Valley and computers, Triumph of the Nerds·(June)

After promising a new OS that it couldn't deliver, Apple seeks a new OS and narrows it down to BeOS(from former Apple executive, Jean-Louis Gassee)and Steve Job's NeXT software.

SJ, in a presentation to Apple's board, convinces it to buy NeXT and its assets for$427 million, with its OS as the major asset. SJ is now back at Apple, albeit in an unofficial advisory capacity. (December)

SJ and Wozniak, after a prolonged absence, return to help reenergize Apple. (January)

1997

Amelio announces that Newton may be dropped from the product line.

Newly minted executive committee members SJ and Wozniak become advisors to Amelio. (February)

Amelio resigns. SJ becomes Apple's interim chief executive, which he terms"iCEO ,"after being offered the CEO position. Citing his continuing interest in Pixar,SJ declines. (July 9)

皮克斯首次公开发行690万股。（11月29日）

吉尔伯特·阿默里奥取代斯平德勒成为苹果新一任CEO，同时出任公司董事会主席。（2月2日）

乔布斯主演了美国国家广播公司拍摄的短剧《小人物的胜利》，讲的是关于硅谷和计算的故事。（7月）

新的OS系统无法按预期发布，苹果寻找到了BeOS系统（苹果前高管简·路易斯·卡西的公司开发的）和乔布斯的NeXT软件作为OS的替代品。

在一次面对苹果公司董事会的演讲中，乔布斯说服了苹果收购NeXT，当时NeXT总价值为2千7百万美元，其中os系统是主要的组成部分。而此时的乔布斯已经以非官方的顾问身份回到了苹果。（12月）

离开多年之后，乔布斯和沃兹终于重回苹果。（1月）

阿梅里奥宣布"牛顿"可能停产。

乔布斯和沃兹作为新加入的理事会成员，成为阿梅里奥的顾问。（2月）

阿梅里奥辞职，此时乔布斯全部的兴趣仍在皮克斯公司，因此婉拒了苹果CEO的任命，成为苹果的临时首席执行官，他自己称之为"iCEO"。（7月9日）

SJ begins the effort to simplify Apple's product line from four dozen computer models to ten.

At Macworld, SJ announces new deals with former business opponent Microsoft, which is met with mixed feelings by Apple followers. (August)

SJ formally announced as Apple's interim CEO. (John Sculley,in a 2010 interview with Leander Kahney, noted: "I'm actually convinced that if Steve hadn't come back when he did—if they had waited another six months--Apple would have been history It would have been gone, absolutely gone. ")(September)

Apple debuts its PowerBook, which runs on the PowerPC G3 chip. (November)

SJ assumes dual CEO responsibilities at Apple and Pixar.

1998

Apple's acquisition of NeXT STEP lays the foundation for its next major software upgrade: Mac OS X, a Unixlike operating system.

At Macworld in San Francisco, Apple announces the Power Mac"Blue and White"G3 tower unit. (January 5)

SJ is featured in PBS's documentary, Nerds 2. 0. 1: A Brief History of the Internet, a follow—up to its Triumph of the Nerds.

乔布斯将苹果的产品线由48条精减到10条。

乔布斯在Macworld大会上宣布了对待微软 —— 苹果之前的商业竞争对手的新政，新政让众多的苹果粉丝们感到喜忧参半。（8月）

乔布斯正式宣布担任苹果的临时CEO。（约翰·斯库利在2010年接受利安得·卡尼采访时曾说："我很确定，如果史蒂夫那时候不回来 —— 如果晚回来六个月 —— 苹果公司就将成为历史，彻底完蛋。"）（9月）

苹果发布PowerBook，继续使用苹果G3处理器。（11月）

乔布斯同时担任苹果和皮克斯两家公司的CEO。

1998

苹果购买了NeXT STEP系统，这个系统成为苹果下一个主要软件 —— Mac OS X的升级基础，这是一个基于Unix的操作系统。

在三藩市召开的苹果大会上，苹果发布了名为Power Mac "Blue and White" G3 的台式机。（1月5日）

乔布斯拍摄了美国国家广播电视公司的短剧《小人物2.0.1：互联网简明史》，是之前《小人物的胜利》的续集。

SJ cleans house at Apple: He significantly decreases the number of products in the competing computer lines, kills numerous projects(notably Newton), kills the software—licensing program, and fires select employees. (March)

Pixar releases A Bug's Life, which grosses$162 million domestically. (November 20)

1999

Apple announces the tray-loading candy-colored iMac G3 in five eye-popping colors and new Power Mac G3 tower units. (January 5)

SJ is depicted in a TV docudrama, portrayed by Noah Wyle, called Pirates of Silicon Valley. (June 20)

Apple debuts the clam—shelled, portable iBook, a pro laptop called the PowerBook G3, and its first wireless network device, the AirPort base station. (July 21)

Pixar releases Toy Story 2, which grosses $245. 8 million domestically. (November 13)

2000

At Macworld, SJ announces that he's dropped his interim CEO status to become permanent CEO. (January 5)

SJ releases Public Beta Mac OS X, built on the bones of NeXT's object-oriented software.

乔布斯在苹果公司进行内部整顿：他缩减了相互矛盾的电脑生产线的数量，停掉了大量项目（值得一提的时，"牛顿"也在其中），中止了软件许可程序的开发，开除了一些优秀的员工。（3月）

皮克斯推出电影《虫虫危机》，美国国内票房收入1亿六千2百万美元。（11月20）

1999

苹果发布了配有托盘式光驱驱动器的iMac G3，iMac G3拥有五种糖果般的绚丽颜色可供选择，同时发布的还有新一代的Power Mac G3台式机。（1月5）

一部讲述乔布斯生平事迹的电视纪录片—《硅谷传奇》拍摄完成，乔布斯扮演者是诺亚·怀尔。（6月20日）

苹果发布了一款拥有蛤壳形状外观的手提电脑—PowerBook G3，它是第一款配有无线上网设备及基站网络更新程序的笔记本电脑（7月21日）

皮克斯推出《玩具总动员2》，美国国内票房收入2亿4千5百8十万美元。（11月13日）

2000

苹果大会上，乔布斯宣布将卸下临时CEO的头衔，成为苹果固定CEO。（1月5日）

史蒂夫发布Mac OS X系统公测版，这版系统是在NeXT面向对象的软件架构基础上开发出来的。

Apple stock falls to$28 a share after the company announces fourth quarter sales will fall"substantially below expectations. "(September 28)

2001

At Macworld, ST shows Mac OS X, "Quicksilver"G4 tower computers, and a titanium PowerBook G4 computer. (January 9)

The first Apple Stores open in Tysons Corner, Virginia, and Glendale, California. (Within a decade, more than 300 such stores opened worldwide.)
(May 19)

Pixar releases Monsters,Inc. , which grosses$255 million domestically. (October 28)

The iPod debuts with the ad line, "1,000 songs in your pocket. "(November 10)

2002

Apple introduces the eMac(education Mac), a line created specifically for the burgeoning educational market. (April 29)

2003

At Macworld, Apple announces the Safari Web browser, iLife software, and new PowerBook models. Later in the month, it also announces new high-end tower units. (January 7)

Pixar releases Finding Nemo, which grosses$339. 7 million domestically. It goes on to win an Academy Award for Best Animated Feature. (May 30)

苹果公司宣布第四季度的销售额将"大大低于预期",随后苹果股价大跌至每股28美元。(9月28日)

苹果大会上展示了Mac OS X系统、"Quicksilver"G4台式机以及钛金属制造的Titanium PowerBook G4。(1月9日)

2001

在维吉尼亚州的泰森角和加州的格林代尔,开设了最早的苹果零售店。(十年之中,苹果零售店的数量增加到300多家,遍布世界各地)。(5月19日)

皮克斯推出《怪兽电力公司》,美国国内票房收入2亿5千5百万美元。(10月28日)

iPod发布,广告语是:"把1000首歌装进口袋"。(11月10日)

苹果发布eMac系列,这条产品线主要面向的是蓬勃发展教育市场。(4月29日)

2002

苹果大会上发布了Safari浏览器、iLife 软件以及新一代PowerBook的样机。当月晚些时候,还发布了一款高端台式电脑。(1月7日)

2003

皮克斯推出《海底总动员》,美国国内票房收入3亿3千9百7十万美元,并且赢得了当年的奥斯卡最佳动画片奖。(5月30日)

Apple debuts the iTunes Music Store for Mac- only computers. (April 28)

Apple debuts the Power Mac G5. (June 24)

The iTunes store opens up to Windows computer users. (October 16)

SJ announces to his employees that he has pancreatic cancer and will have to undergo an operation to remove a tumor. Taking a medical leave of absence, SJ turns the reins over to Apple's head of worldwide sales and operations, Timothy D. Cook. (August)

2004

Early in the years SJ's acrimonious dealings with Disney's CEO, Michael Eisner, created what looked to be an impassable rift regarding Pixar. SJ courts other studios, which show great interest in a partnership.

Disney CEO Michael Eisner is ousted by the board, a move orchestrated by board member Roy Disney's"Save Disney"campaign. Eisner is replaced by Disney's chief operating officer, Robert Iger,who sees Pixar aS the future of Disney animation. (September)

Pixar releases The Incredible, which grosses$261 million domestically. It goes on to win an Academy Award for Best Animated Feature. (November 5)

Apple introduces the Mac Mini computer at Macworld Expo in San Francisco.

2005

苹果推出iTunes音乐商店，只面向Mac用户提供服务。（4月28日）

苹果推出Power Mac G5。（6月24日）

iTunes音乐商店对Windows电脑用户开放。（10月16日）

乔布斯对员工宣布自己患上胰腺癌，为了接受肿瘤切除手术，将请病假休息。并将职权交给了苹果全球销售和运营总监蒂姆·库克。（8月）

同年早些时候，乔布斯和迪斯尼CEO迈克尔·艾斯纳交恶，皮克斯中止了和迪斯尼的合作，乔布斯另觅新欢，找到了一家表现出极大诚意的工作室。

迪斯尼董事会成员罗伊·迪斯尼领导了一场名为"拯救迪斯尼"的运动，董事会罢免了CEO迈克尔·艾斯纳，由首席运营官罗伯特·伊戈尔接任CEO一职，伊戈尔将皮克斯视为迪斯尼动画的未来和希望。（9月）

皮克斯推出《超人特攻队》，美国国内票房收入2亿6千1百万美元，并且赢得了当年的奥斯卡最佳动画片奖。（11月5日）

在三藩市召开的麦金塔世界博览会上，苹果推出了Mac Mini电脑。

Apple develops an Intel version of Mac OS X as it prepares a permanent switch from the PowerPC platform to an Intel platform. Using Apple's new"Boot Camp"software, Windows programs will soon run on the Mac.

2006

Disney buys Pixar for$7. 4 billion; SJ gets a 7%stake ($3. 5 billion) in Disney, becoming its largest individual shareholder. He also becomes a member of its board of directors. (January 24)

Apple debuts the Mac Book(May 16)

and a tower unit, the Mac Pro. (August 7)

Pixar releases Cars, which grosses$244 million domestically. (June 9)

SJ's gaunt-looking appearance at the annual Apple Worldwide Developers Conference(WWDC)gives rise to speculation regarding his health and Apple's succession plans. SJ announces OS X 10. 5 Leopard.

2007

SJ announces at the Macworld Expo that he is repositioning Apple Computer Inc. , as, simply, Apple, Inc. (January 9)

Apple debuts the original iPhone.

Apple debuts its Apple TV at Macworld. (February)

苹果开始研发英特尔版本的Mac OS X，似乎准备从PowerPC平台永远转移至英特尔平台。装上苹果新开发的Boot Camp软件后，Windows下的程序可以马上在Mac上运行。

2006

迪斯尼以74亿美元的价格收购了皮克斯公司，乔布斯获得了迪斯尼公司7%的股份（价值35亿美元），成为最大的个人股东，同时也成为董事会成员。（1月24日）

苹果发布MacBook。（5月16日）

以及Mac Pro台式机，Mac Pro。（8月7日）

皮克斯推出《汽车总动员》，美国国内票房2亿4千4百万美元。（6月9日）

乔布斯一脸憔悴的亮相一年一度的苹果电脑全球研发者大会，一时间关于他健康状况及苹果"接班人计划"的猜测甚嚣尘上。乔布斯发布OS X 10.5 Leopard。

2007

乔布斯在麦金塔世界博览会上宣布将苹果电脑公司的名称简化为苹果公司。（1月9日）

苹果发布第一代iPhone。

苹果在麦金塔世界博览会上发布苹果TV。（2月）

Pixar releases Ratatouille, which grosses$206 million domestically. It goes on to win an Academy Award for Best Animated Feature Film. (June 29)

SJ is inducted into the California Museum's Hall of Fame by Governor Arnold Schwarzenegger. (December 5)

Apple announces at Macworld the MacBook Air, a lightweight laptop. (January 15)

Pixar releases WALL·E, which grosses$223 domestically. It goes on to win an Academy Award for Best Animated Feature. (June 27)

SJ's appearance at the WWDC prompts renewed concerns about his health. Later that month, Bloomberg prematurely releases SJ's obituary. At an Apple event SJ quotes Mark Twain, "Reports of my death are greatly exaggerated. "(September 9)

SJ announces to his employees, in an interoffice memo, that he is taking a six-month medical leave due to health issues. In his absence, Timothy Cook once again takes over as acting CEO. (January 14)

At Methodist University Hospital Transplant Institute in Memphis, SJ undergoes a successful liver transplant·(April)

Pixar releases Up which grosses$293 million domestically. It goes on to win two Academy Awards(Best Achievement in Music Written for Motion Pictures, Original Score and Best Animated Feature Film). (May29)

皮克斯推出《料理鼠王》，美国国内票房2亿零6百万美元，并获得了当年奥斯卡最佳动画影片奖。（6月29日）

乔布斯受加州州长阿诺·施瓦辛格之邀，入驻加州名人堂。（12月5日）

2008

苹果在麦金塔世界博览会上发布了轻便的手提电脑——MacBook Air。（1月15日）

皮克斯推出《机器人总动员》，美国国内票房2亿2千3百万美元，并获得了当年奥斯卡最佳动画影片奖。（6月27日）

乔布斯亮相全球开发者大会，再度引发了人们对他健康问题的关注。当月晚些时候，彭博社草率发布乔布斯的讣告，对此，乔布斯引用了马克·吐温的话，"关于我的死亡的报道都太言过其实了。"（9月9日）

2009

乔布斯向苹果员工宣布，由于健康原因，他将休病假六个月，在休假期间，蒂姆·库克会再次代替他担任CEO一职。（1月14日）

在田纳西孟菲斯的卫理公会大学医院移植研究所，乔布斯接受了成功的肝移植手术。（4月）

皮克斯推出《飞屋环游记》，美国国内票房2亿9千3百万美元，并获得了当年奥斯卡最佳动画长片及最佳原创音乐两项大奖。（5月29日）

Fortune magazine names SJ the "CEO of the decade."

2010

Pixar releases Toy Story 3, which grosses$415 million domestically. It goes on to win two Academy Awards (Best Achievement in Music Written for Motion Pictures, Original Song and Best Animated Feature Film)(June 18)

Apple debuts the iPad, ushering in the tablet era (April 3).

SJ creates an organ donors registry. (October)

Financial Times names SJ as its "Person of the Year. "

2011

Apple opens the Mac App store. (January 6)

SJ takes an extended, open—ended leave of absence and again, Timothy Cook takes the helm. SJ remains involved in strategic decisions. (January 17)

After years of contentious talks with the local town council in Woodside, California, SJ finally gets approval to demolish his mansion to construct an$8. 45 million. 4, 910-square foot home, about which architect Christopher Travis remarked to Wired magazine, "The site plan definitely shows unnatural restraint for a person of wealth. This kind of thing only happens when the client gives the architect specific instructions to be sparse and utilitarian. "(February)

Apple sells iPad 2. (March 11)

乔布斯被《财富》杂志选为"十年最佳首席执行官"。

2010

皮克斯推出《玩具总动员3》，美国国内票房4亿1千5百万美元，并获得了当年奥斯卡最佳动画长片及最佳原创音乐两项大奖。（6月18日）

苹果发布iPad，宣告平板电脑时代到来。（4月3日）

乔布斯进行器官捐赠登记。（10月）

《金融时报》授予乔布斯"年度风云人物"称号。

2011

苹果的Mac应用商店开业。（1月6日）

乔布斯宣布延长休假时间，且没有具体时限，蒂姆·库克再次掌舵苹果。乔布斯仍然参与战略决策的制定工作。（1月17日）

在和加州伍德赛德市议会多年谈判之后，议会终于批准了乔布斯拆除原有住宅的申请，这所房子总面积4910平方公尺，价值845万美元，建筑师克里斯托弗·特拉维斯在《连线杂志》中这样评论到："该建筑规划绝对显示了有钱人的非本性约束。这种事情只会发生在客户向建筑师发出具体指示，要求实用和简约时。我可以说这个规划是由乔布斯特别要求的结果，即要求平淡和简单。"（2月）

苹果开始出售iPad 2。（3月11日）

Pixar releases Cars 2, which grosses$189 million domestically(as of September 15, 2011). (June 24)

Mac OS 10. 7, Lion, is released, bringing the look and feel of the iPhone and iPad iOS to Apple's computer line. It is available only by download as an Apple application for$29. 99. (July 20)

Based on Apple's market capitalization of$343 billion ($371. 66 per share), it temporarily exceeds Exxon's market cap as the world's most valuable company. (August)

Apple submits a new proposal to the Cupertino City Council to build a new campus designed by Foster+Partners. Dubbed"the Spaceship"because of its round design, it will be built on 98 acres of land and be completed in 2015.

Steve Jobs, the only authorized biography of SJ, written by Walter Isaacson, moves up its publication date from March 6, 2012 to November 21, 2011. (August 15)

Steve Jobs resigns as CEO from Apple. Timothy Cook is appointed CEO as SJ assumes the position of chairman. (August 24)

Apple CEO Timothy Cook holds his first media event to announce the iPhone 4GS. (October 4)

Steve Jobs dies. (October 5)

皮克斯推出《汽车总动员2》，截止到2011年9月15日，美国国内票房1亿8千9百万美元。（6月24日）

Mac OS 10.7，Lion发布，该系统将iPhone和iPad iOS的操作界面和感觉引入了苹果电脑产品线。该系统只能够以苹果应用软件程序的形式付费下载，费用为29.99美元。（7月20日）

苹果以3430亿美元的股票总市值（每股371.66美元），超越了艾克森石油公司，成为世界上最值钱的公司。（8月）

苹果向库比蒂诺市议会提交了一项议案，申请建造一所新大楼，大楼由英国福斯特建筑师傅所担任总设计，因为其圆形的外观结构，起名为"宇宙飞船"，占地98英亩，2015年完工。

史蒂夫·乔布斯的唯一授权个人传记，由沃尔特·艾萨克森编写完成。出版日期由2012年3月3日提前到2011年11月21日。（8月15日）

史蒂夫·乔布斯辞去苹果CEO一职。蒂姆·库克被任命为CEO，同时加入苹果公司董事会。（8月24日）

苹果CEO蒂姆·库克主持iPhone 4GS的发布会，这也是他上任后的第一次面对媒体亮相。（10月4日）

史蒂夫·乔布斯去世。（10月5日）

END OF AN ERA

一个时代的终结

图书在版编目（CIP）数据

乔布斯自述 / (美) 乔布斯著；巨澜, 李墨林译.
— 北京: 中国时代经济出版社, 2012.4
书名原文: Steve Jobs by Steve Jobs
ISBN 978-7-5119-1076-9

Ⅰ.①乔… Ⅱ.①乔… ②巨… ③李…
Ⅲ.①乔布斯，S.（1955~2011）– 自传 Ⅳ.①K837.125.38

中国版本图书馆CIP数据核字(2012)第041492号

书　　名：乔布斯自述
作　　者：乔布斯
译　　者：巨澜　李墨林

出版发行：中国时代经济出版社
社　　址：北京市丰台区玉林里25号楼
邮政编码：100069
发行热线：（010）68351353　68320825
传　　真：（010）68320634　68320484
网　　址：www.cmepub.com.cn
电子邮箱：zgsdjj@hotmail.com
经　　销：各地新华书店
印　　刷：北京毅峰迅捷印刷有限公司
开　　本：32
字　　数：190千字
印　　张：8
版　　次：2012年4月第1版
印　　次：2012年4月第1次印刷
书　　号：ISBN 978-7-5119-1076-9
定　　价：32.80元
